WASHINGTON
A CHRONOLOGICAL & DOCUMENTARY HISTORY

1790-1970

Compiled and Edited by
HOWARD B. FURER

Series Editor
HOWARD B. FURER

PAL

1975
OCEANA PUBLICATIONS, INC.
Dobbs Ferry, New York

Library of Congress Cataloging in Publication Data

Furer, Howard B   1934-
    Washington, a chronological & documentary history,
1790-1970.

    (American cities chronology series)
    Bibliography: p.
    Includes index.
    SUMMARY: Presents a chronology of important events in
the history of Washington, D.C., accompanied by pertinent
documents.
    1. Washington, D.C. -- History--Chronology. 2. Wash-
ington, D.C.--History--Sources. [1. Washington, D.C.
--History] I. Title.
F194.F87   975.3   74-30371
ISBN 0-379-00611-1

TABLE OF CONTENTS

EDITOR'S FOREWORD

The purpose of this book is to provide the interested student with a concise picture of the history, growth, and development of the Nation's Capital. This work does not presume to be the definitive study on Washington, D.C. However, despite its limitations of size, this small volume can provide the reader with a good starting point to pursue his study of the subject further. Obviously, much more could have been included in the chronology, documents, and bibliography sections of this work. As a result, some aspects of Washington's growth and development have not been fully treated, while others have been ignored. Despite these shortcomings, this work attempts to present as well rounded a picture of the city as is possible in a book of this size. Every attempt has been made to cite the most accurate dates in the chronology section. However, in case of a conflict, the student is urged to go to the original sources.

In essence, then, this study is a research tool intended to guide the reader toward an initial understanding of this fascinating topic. Because the very nature of preparing a chronology of this type precludes the author from using the standard form of historical footnoting, I should like to acknowledge, in the editor's foreword, the major sources used to compile the bulk of the chronological and factual materials comprising the chronology section of this work. Constance McLaughlin Green's Pulitzer Prize winning two volume study on the history of the Nation's Capital, Washington, Village and Capital, 1800-1878 (Princeton University Press, Princeton, New Jersey, 1962), and Washington, Capital City, 1879-1950 (Princeton University Press, Princeton, New Jersey, 1963), proved invaluable in in gathering the facts and dates used for large sections of the chronology. My grateful thanks go to Mrs. Nora H. Bangs, Permissions Manager of Princeton University Press, who read the chronology, and granted me permission to cite Mrs. Green's two books in this foreword. Other books used in preparing the chronology were; Wilhelmus B. Bryan, A History of the National Capital, 2 vols., (New York, 1914-1916), Federal Writer's Project, Washington: City and Capital (Washington, D.C., 1937), and Washington League of Women Voters, Washington, D.C.; A Tale of Two Cities (Washington, D.C., 1962). My especial thanks go to Ms. Roxanna Henson of the Washingtoniana Division of the District of Columbia Public Library for her invaluable aid in seeking out many of the documents used in this work.

Howard B. Furer
Kean College of New Jersey
Union, New Jersey

THE FIRST FIFTY YEARS OF WASHINGTON'S DEVELOPMENT
1790-1840

1790   Alexander Hamilton and Thomas Jefferson arranged a com-
                promise for the site of the federal city.. In return for
                Hamilton's securing Northern support for a Southern capi-
                tal, Jefferson agreed to support Hamilton's plan for the
                federal assumption of state debts.

                July 16. Congress passed the Residence Act allowing the
                President to choose a location for the capital city some-
                where along the Potomac River. He was also to choose
                three commissioners, surveyors, and an architect. The
                federal constitution provided for a federal city outside the
                jurisdiction of any one state.

1791   January. President George Washington chose land near
                Georgetown, which had been laid out in 1751 and incorpor-
                ated in 1789, for the capital city. At the same time, he
                named the commissioners, appointed Andrew Ellicott as
                surveyor, and Pierre Charles L'Enfant as architect.

                March 3. The Residence Act was amended.

                September. The Board of Capital Commissioners named
                the federal city Washington. It, along with Alexandria
                (ceded by the government of Virginia) and Georgetown
                (ceded by the government of Maryland) was called the Dis-
                trict of Columbia.

                September 24. The Board of Capital Commissioners tried
                to sell lots in the city by means of an auction, in order to
                raise money for the erection of public buildings. The auc-
                tion proved unsuccessful.

1792   The construction of the Executive Mansion (the White House)
                began.

                February. President Washington fired Pierre L'Enfant as
                chief architect and engineer of the city. Andrew Ellicott
                was instructed to draw a map of the city for use at another
                public auction of town lots. Ellicott hired a free black,
                Benjamin Banneker, as surveyor for the job.

                October. Another public auction to sell lots in the city
                again proved unsuccessful.

1793   The Board of Capital Commissioners, in order to build the
                Capitol and other government buildings, sold 3000 lots in
                the city to a syndicate of James Greenleaf, Robert Morris,
                and James Nicholson.

                March. The construction of the Capitol began.

1796   Pennsylvania Avenue was laid out.

1797   The Greenleaf, Morris, Nicholson syndicate went bankrupt.

                May. Thomas Law came to the city. He was Washington's
                first manufacturer. He established a sugar refinery near
                Greenleaf's Point.

1798   Ninety slaves made up the work force building the Capitol.

1800   Washington's population numbered, 3,244,623 of them black
                slaves. The District of Columbia held 14,093 inhabitants.

                June 3. The seat of government was officially established
                in the city. President John Adams was met at the District
                line and escorted to the city's Union Tavern.

                August. The first theater in the city opened, but closed a
                month later.

                Washington contained 109 brick houses and 263 wooden
                houses.

                August 15. The Board of Capital Commissioners cut the
                price of city lots in order to raise money and to attract re-
                sidents. This scheme was successful.

                September. The first newspapers in Washington began
                publication. They were the National Intelligencer, the Uni-
                versal Gazette, the Washington Federalist, and the Museum.
                Most of them were short-lived, but the Intelligencer lasted
                until 1869. The first publisher was Samuel Harrison Smith.

                October. The Library of Congress was founded.

                November 1. Congress placed the president in charge of
                the District of Columbia. Judicial authority was based on
                the Maryland system.

November 17. Congress met for the first time in Washington.

December 1. Congress passed an act stating that District residents did not have the right to vote in national elections or have representation in Congress.

1801   The Bank of the United States opened a branch in the city of Washington.

April. The State and War Department Buildings were completed.

May. Congress established a judiciary for the District of Columbia.

September. The "Oven," a room for the meetings of the House of Representatives was added to the uncompleted Capitol Building.

December. The Board of Capital Commissioners held two public land auctions in the city, but neither raised very much money.

1802   Government engineers completed a series of canals and locks around the falls above Georgetown to facilitate the federal city's commercial activity.

May. Congress granted the federal city a charter. A local white resident who owned at least one hundred dollars worth of property had the right to elect a city council. He could not, however, vote for president, vice-president, or a district representative in Congress.

June 1. The president appointed Robert Brent as the first mayor of Washington.

June 6. Washingtonians elected their first city council.

1803   January 10. Washington property owners asked Congress for a territorial type of government. The request was denied.

1804   Washington's charter was amended to make both branches of its council elective.

August 22. Congress allowed the city government to establish schools.

December 5. The city passed a measure giving $1500 a year to a board of elected trustees for the maintenance of schools.

1805

The city council levied a luxury tax on wine and whiskey, slaves, and carriages. The proceeds went for the support of two schools.

Taxes were paid for paving the streets, highways, and bridges. In 1805, $4,500 out of $9,000 collected in taxes and license fees went for these purposes as Congress refused to appropriate any money for this vital urban service.

April. A resolution to free slaves in the District of Columbia when they reached maturity was defeated by Congress.

August 7. President Thomas Jefferson, Mayor Brent, Thomas Tingery, William Cranch, Samuel Harrison Smith, and eight other citizens became trustees of the "Permanent Institution for the Education of Youth," the city's public Board of Education.

1806

The leading manufacturing establishment in the city was the navy yard. In 1806 it employed 175 workmen at a salary of $1.81 a day.

February. The Western School opened on Pennsylvania Avenue between 17th and 18th Streets. It was the first public school in the city with its own building.

May 16. The Eastern School opened on First Street. Black children were excluded from both public schools by de facto segregation.

May 28. St. Patrick's Roman Catholic Church on F Street was dedicated.

1807

Congress appropriated $3,000 for repairs to the thoroughfares from the Treasury to the Capitol and for the planting of Lombardy Poplar trees along this avenue.

June. The first black school in the city opened. It was taught by a white man.

August 5. The Episcopalian Christ Church, designed by
Benjamin Latrobe, was completed on Southeast G Street.

1808   By 1808, some congressmen wished to move the capital tal
              to Philadelphia.

              March. The South Wing of the Capitol and the Senate Wing
              were completed under the direction of Benjamin Latrobe.
              Guiseppi Franzoni and Giovanni Andrei carved the stone-
              work of the building's interior.

              June 20. Mayor Brent called a public meeting to set up a
              company to manufacture cotton, wool, hemp, and flax.

              July 13. Samuel Harrison Smith, Cornelius Coningham, and
              William Cranch established the Columbia Manufacturing
              Company in the city. It went out of business before 1813.

              September. Washington did not have a water works. The
              city dug wells in the public squares. Only a few residents
              had water piped into their homes.

              December 6. The mayor and council of Washington enacted
              the city's first black code. It was moderate by Southern
              standards.

1809   The first bridge across the Potomac River from Maryland
              Avenue to Alexandria, Virgina, was constructed.

              By 1809, there were five banks in the District of Columbia.

              May 23. The city poorhouse was built at 6th and M Streets.

1810   The population of Washington was 8,209, while that of the
              District of Columbia was 24,023.

              Work began on the construction of the Washington Canal.

              Congress granted the banks of the District more liberal
              charters and greater credit resources.

              A causeway from Analoostan Island to the Virginia shore
              was constructed. A dam was also built.

              February. The Washington Benevolent Society of Young
              Men was organized.

1811   May 31. Mayor Brent doubled the size of Washington's po-
            lice force from one to two officers.

            September 28. The Washington Library Company was foun-
            ded.

            December. An attempt was made to void the property quali-
            fications for voting in the city. It failed.

1812   May 5. Two Lancastrian schools opened with money raised
            by a lottery.

            June 16. The War of 1812 began. The city lacked proper
            defenses.

            September 10. Washingtonians, too old for militia duty,
            formed a company of volunteers to defend the city.

            December. Washington received a new charter from con-
            gress. The mayor was to be chosen by a new twenty-man
            council, elected by the voters in the four wards into which
            the city was divided.

            December 16. The city council, with Congressional appro-
            val, ordered six month jail sentences for disorderly free
            blacks and mulattoes and forty lashes for slaves. The coun-
            cil also required every free black to register and carry a
            certificate of freedom.

1813   July 17. Mayor James Blake appointed a night watch to pa-
            trol the streets.

1814   Black Methodists built the Mt. Zion Negro Church, the first
            black church in the city.

            January 26. The Bank of the Metropolis opened in the city.

            February 26. A lottery was held in the city to raise money
            for building a monument to George Washington.

            June 19. British troops from Admiral George Cockburn's
            ships were 22 miles from Washington.

            July 25. Secretary of War John Armstrong made plans for
            the defense of the city.

August 24. The British army captured the city. Most of the public buildings were burned, but on the night of August 25, the British withdrew from Washington.

September 2. President and Mrs. James Madison returned to the city. They moved into the Octagon House on New York Avenue, as the White House had been destroyed.

September 19. Congress rejected a bill to move the Capital out of Washington. The city's bankers gave a $500,000 loan to the government to rebuild the public buildings.

1815   The city council combined the poorhouse with the workhouse.

Congress granted a charter to Georgetown Seminary allowing it to award degrees.

February 17. President Madison signed the Treaty of Ghent, ending the War of 1812, at the Octagon House.

March. New Capital Commissioners were appointed to see to the rebuilding of the city following its destruction during the War of 1812.

May 7. Thomas Law, Daniel Carroll, and others began construction of a building in which Congress could meet until the Capitol was rebuilt. The 14th Congress convened in this building in December.

June 6. The Columbia Typographical Union was founded in the city. It was the first union in Washington and one of the first working men's organizations in the country.

November. The Washington Canal was opened. It was not very successful in stimulating trade for the city.

November 28. The Washington City Orphan Asylum was founded on Northwest 10th Street by Marcia Burnes Van Ness, Mrs. Obadiah Brown, Mrs. Samuel Harrison Smith, and Dolly Madison.

1816   June 28. The city council voted $1,500 from taxes for schools in the first district, and $600 from taxes for schools in the second district.

August 15. John Quincy Adams, Josiah Meigs, Benjamin

Latrobe, and Edward Cutbush founded the Columbian Institute for the "promotion of the arts and sciences."

1817   The Washington Botanical Society was founded.

The Medical Society of the District of Columbia was organized.

March. Congress renewed all the old bank charters in the
city and granted new charters to six unincorporated banks
within the District.

March 4. James Monroe was inaugurated President on the
steps of the "Brick Capitol" building.

August 23. St. John's Church was constructed by Benjamin
Latrobe.

September. The new White House was completed. President and Mrs. James Monroe were the first to reside in the
building.

1818   Congress chartered the Columbian Institute and gave it six
acres of land at the foot of Capitol Hill for a botanical garden.

The city council reduced the amount of money that the first
and second wards might use from taxes for schools to
$1,000.

June. The Franklin Fire Insurance Company was incorporated in Washington.

July 10. A free school for black children was opened by the
Colored Resolute Beneficial Society. It received no municipal aid.

July 11. The city began to build water reservoirs to be used
to fight fires. Economy stopped this plan in 1819.

December 11. President Monroe reintroduced the plan of
territorial status for the District. The plan was debated,
but no action was taken for eight years.

1819   The Decatur House, built by Benjamin Latrobe for Commo-
dore Stephen Decatur, was completed.

February. The Panic of 1819 severely affected the District. However, government activities kept Washington from feeling the full force of the nationwide depression.

November 29. Congress spent $4,500 for two fire engines, the construction of one fire house near the Capitol, and another near the White House.

December. The Capitol Building was completed.

1820   The population of Washington was 13,117, while the population of the District as a whole stood at 33,039, including 3,000 free blacks.

Blacks in Washington formed the African Methodist Episcopal Church, the first independent black church in the city.

May 15. Washington received a new charter with greater powers in all municipal affairs. The right to elect the mayor was the most important change.

June 1. Six wards were created out of the original four. The second and third wards were the wealthiest.

July 8. The city hired public scavengers to make regular rounds to improve sanitation in Washington. These officials, however, were inefficient, and garbage collection depended on the efforts of private citizens.

August 22. The cornerstone of the new City Hall was laid. John Law was the dedication speaker.

1821   Baptists opened the Columbian College, which became a university in 1873, and later George Washington University.

May 22. The Washington Theater was destroyed by fire.

July 21. Congress granted banks in the District new fifteen year charters.

1822   May. Gaetoni Carusi and his son established the Assembly Rooms, which became the city's chief public gathering place.

June. Thomas Carberry, the poor man's candidate, was elected mayor. Carberry immediately enrolled on the assessment books the names of men who owned no property, and for a while property qualifications for voting were abolished.

October 30. A Washington town meeting established and promised to finance the Female Orphan Asylum.

1823   Congress contributed $10,000 to the building of the City Hall.

November. A convention was called to meet in Washington to discuss the construction of the Potomac Canal, which, it was believed, would enable the city to tap the trade of the Ohio Valley. This was the beginning of the Chesapeake and Ohio Canal.

1824   The Blair House was built by Joseph Lovell. It was purchased by Francis Preston Blair in 1836, and by the United States government in 1943.

May 22. The city council reestablished property qualifications for voting.

November 16. The Howard Charity Society was organized. It was headed by Samuel Southard, William Seaton, and William A. Bradley.

1825   Lafayette Square was built.

The Potomac Company went bankrupt. The Chesapeake and Ohio Company was chartered to build a canal to the Ohio River, and Congress invested $1,000,000 in the company. The District of Columbia invested $1,500,000.

January 14. A second city orphanage was opened with the Sisters of Charity and Father Matthews of St. Patrick's Church in charge.

December 31. The Washington City Orphan Asylum opened. The site was donated by John and Marcia Van Ness.

1826   Congress appropriated $5,000 for repairs to the Washington City Jail.

The Washington Society for the Abolition of Slavery in the District of Columbia was formed.

July 27. The school board held lotteries that raised about

$40,000. The mayor invested the $40,000 in 6 percent bonds and used two-thirds of the income to support two public pauper schools.

1827   Father Vanlomen founded the first seminary for black girls in the District.

January 22. The Federal Prison in the city was completed.

May 31. The city enacted a new black code restricting the activities of blacks in Washington even more than earlier.

1828   Congress ordered the Commissioner of Public Buildings in Washington to bar blacks from the Capitol except when they were there on business.

Eleven hundred petitions were sent to Congress to end slavery in the District of Columbia.

July 4. Construction began on the Chesapeake and Ohio Canal. At the same time, the Baltimore and Ohio Railroad was begun, financed in part with money from Washington merchants and bankers. Neither of these projects proved successful.

December. Joseph Gales was elected mayor.

1829   Federal building programs stopped and did not begin again until the mid 1830s.

January. A severe influenza epidemic struck the city.

March 4. Andrew Jackson was inaugurated president. After the speech, a mob of his followers "invaded the White House reception, tore the drapes, broke the furniture, and trampled the expensive carpets."

December. The District cities financed their purchase of stock in the Chesapeake and Ohio Canal by means of a $1,500,000 loan from Dutch banks.

1830   The population of Washington reached 18,826, while that of the District as a whole stood at 39,834.

Many auctions took place in the city during the year as anti-Jacksonians left Washington, leaving their goods behind.

Benjamin Lundy, an abolitionist, began publishing the Genius of Universal Emancipation in Washington.

Beginning in 1830, the social structure of the city changed as a result of the "Jacksonian revolution."

April. Penal reform began in the District, and a new criminal code was enacted; prison replaced the death penalty for most capital crimes.

August 26. The Washington Relief Society was founded by John McLeod.

October 28. The Association of Mechanics of the City of Washington was formed.

December. John Van Ness was elected mayor.

1831   The city began widening and deepening the Washington Canal.

September. The first part of the Chesapeake and Ohio Canal was opened, linking the Potomac River with Rock Creek through the first locks of the canal.

1832   Pennsylvania Avenue was macadamized, President's Square was graded, and water was piped into the Capitol.

Congress gave $25,000 in city lots to Columbian College.

March. Georgetown enacted a black code, the first in its history.

August 8-September 29. A severe epidemic of Asiatic cholera hit Washington.

December. William Bradley was elected mayor.

1833   The Bank of the Metropolis was chosen as one of President Jackson's "pet banks" after government deposits had been withdrawn from the Bank of the United States.

The Treasury was burned to the ground.

By 1833 the city found it very hard to pay the interest on the Dutch loan, and by 1836 it had fallen into arrears on her interest payments.

February. Samuel Southard delivered a report to Congress which stated that the national capital was the concern of the entire country and that federal spending in the city was justified.

August 28. Congress built a causeway at the foot of 14th Street and constructed a toll free Long Bridge across the Potomac River.

August 28-September 15. A race riot against blacks in the city took place. It began as a result of tension caused by abolitionist literature and speakers and was known as the "Snow Storm."

September 21. The city council passed new ordinances prohibiting the issuance of shop-licenses to free blacks in the city, and toughened its black code.

November. The first Baltimore and Ohio Railroad branch line reached the outskirts of Washington.

December 7. The National Theater in Washington opened. Joseph Jefferson was the star of the theater's first production.

1836   Construction began on a new Treasury Building at the old site. Robert Mills was chosen as architect for the new structure.

An Englishman, James Smithson, gave his entire estate to the United States of America to establish in Washington an institution for the "increase and diffusion of knowledge among men." This was the beginning of the Smithsonian Institution.

May. The federal government assumed the District's $1,500,000 canal debts.

December. Peter Force was elected mayor.

December 5. In order to get men to serve in the volunteer fire companies, Congress passed an act exempting such men from militia duty and allowed them to buy insurance at low rates. These schemes did not prove successful.

December 13. The Post Office Building was destroyed by fire. During 1837, construction began on a new one on E and 7th Streets.

1837   By 1837, the attitude of the majority of Washingtonians to-
                ward slavery had changed. They stopped sending petitions
                to Congress for prohibition of the slave trade, approved the
                "gag rule" in Congress, and vehemently resented any out-
                side interference in their slavery problem.

                The improved Washington Canal opened and brought a meas-
                ure of prosperity to Washington and Georgetown.

                February. When the Panic of 1837 struck the country,
                Washington was hardly touched as a result of federal spend-
                ing in the city.

1838   Congress renewed the charters of seven banks in the Dis-
                trict after the Panic of 1837 caused a number of them to
                shut down.

                December. Peter Force was reelected mayor.

                December 17. The Female Union Benevolent Society was
                organized in Washington.

1840   The population of the city reached 23,364, while that of the
                District was 43,712.

                The National Institute for the Promotion of Science was foun-
                ded in Washington under the leadership of Joel Poinsett.

                By 1840, there were four independent black church congre-
                gations in Washington.

                Washington's attempt to limit the black population of the city
                was futile. By 1840 there were 4,800 free blacks in Wash-
                ington, although the city had 600 fewer slaves than ten years
                before.

                July 7. The Charter of 1820 was renewed for another eight
                years, although groups of Washingtonians asked for a new
                charter granting greater political recognition and the re-
                moval of property qualifications for voting.

                December 2. William Winston Seaton was elected mayor.

                WASHINGTON MATURES - 1841-1865

1841   March 4. The most elaborate parade the city had ever staged took place during the inauguration of William Henry Harrison.

August 25. A drunken crowd, angry at President John Tyler because of his veto of a bank bill, gathered at the portico of the White House to jeer him.

1842   Congress incorporated the National Institute in the city.

By 1842 Washington had six volunteer fire companies.

September 3. Congress established an auxiliary guard, which, for the first time in the city's history, provided regular nighttime policing.

November 14. Mayor Seaton asked the city council to enact a special tax to make free schooling available to all white children in Washington. Nothing came of his school plan for two years.

December. Mayor Seaton was reelected.

1843   Horatio Greenough completed his statue of George Washington after nine years of work. It was placed on the east lawn of the Capitol grounds.

Work began on a series of buildings at Marine Hospital Square for a new asylum which would include an infirmary, an almshouse, and a workhouse.

John F. Cook was ordained Washington's first black Presbyterian minister.

February. The city council passed an ordinance making the public schools in Washington free to all white children.

May 10. A new jail was constructed in the city.

November 1. The city council enacted Sunday closing ordinances in a move to reduce violence in the city.

1844   October 8. The National Observatory in Washington was opened.

December 4. William W. Seaton won reelection for a third term as mayor.

December 6. The city council accepted Mayor Seaton's plan to allow the city to build at least one new school from public funds, open all the city schools to all white children, rich and poor, and charge fifty cents a month tuition for any child whose parents could pay.

March 5. The National Theater burned to the ground.

May 26. The Washington Infirmary opened.

August 4. The new school board, composed of twelve members, three men appointed from each of the four districts, was created.

1846   Street lamps were placed along Pennsylvania Avenue.

May. Washington businessmen organized a national fair.

May 13. War with Mexico was declared. Washington's merchants and bankers profited from war contracts.

August 10. Congress acted to fulfill James Smithson's will. A bill was passed appointing regents and authorizing the construction of a building for the Smithsonian Institution. Joseph Henry was appointed its first secretary.

September 7. An act of Congress reduced by one-third the size of the District of Columbia by retroceding Alexandria to the state of Virginia. At the same time, Congress refused Georgetown's request to be reannexed by Maryland.

December 4. Mayor Seaton was reelected for a fourth time.

1847   March 3. Congress authorized the installation of a sixteen foot lantern on a seventy-five foot pole on top of the Capitol dome.

May 1. The cornerstone of the Smithsonian Institution was laid. James Renfrew was the architect.

1848   The government bought the Benning's and Navy Yard Bridges over the Eastern Branch of the Potomac. Washingtonians believed that free bridges would revive the tobacco trade with Maryland. No appreciable gains were made.

February 2. The Treaty of Guadalupe-Hidalgo ending the

Mexican War was signed. Congressional debates over slavery and the slave trade in the District of Columbia and the
nation resumed.

March 24. Dr. Gamliel Bailey began publishing the National
Era in Washington, an anti-slavery newspaper.

May 6. The Washington Gas Light Company was organized.

May 27. A new city charter went into effect. Property
qualifications for voting were ended.

June 17. Mayor Seaton was reelected for a fifth term.

July 4. The cornerstone for the Washington Monument was
laid. Robert Mills was appointed architect.

1849   A boat basin was built on the Potomac and new appropriations
were voted by Congress for docks and piers.

A cholera epidemic struck the city, claiming a mortality
rate of 35 per 1,000.

January. Abraham Lincoln, congressman from Illinois,
proposed the abolition of slavery in the District of Columbia.

February 2. Congress appropriated $20,000 to clear the
city canal where it passed through public grounds. The city
began to dredge the rest of the three mile stretch.

February 7. The city council issued a statement in which
they opposed the slave trade in the city.

August 6. Mayor Seaton appointed ward sanitary committees to aid the Board of Health. Lime was spread over the
stagnant pools in the city to prevent the breeding of mosqui-
toes and disease.

November 17. The Washington Teacher's Institute was
formed at the suggestion of Joseph Henry.

1850   The population of Washington reached 40,001. The total
population of the District was 51,687.

By 1850 blacks made up 26 percent of the city's population.

By 1850 representatives and senators brought their families to Washington to live during the Congressional sessions.

The Chesapeake and Ohio Canal reached Cumberland, Maryland, but no increase in Washington's business activity occurred.

March. Councilman Jesse E. Dow urged the city government to establish black public schools. No action was taken.

June. Walter Lenox was elected mayor.

September 20. An act, abolishing the slave trade in the District of Columbia, was passed by Congress.

October. The city council reexamined local ordinances concerning free blacks in the city and passed a series of amendments to the city's black code, which tightened restrictions on black residents.

1851   Myrtilla Miner opened a high school for "colored girls."

March 11. A salaried police department was established for the city. The size of the force was substantially increased.

July 4. The cornerstone for the extension of the Capitol (two large wings and a huge new dome) was laid.

December 27. Fire destroyed the Library of Congress in the main building of the Capitol.

1852   By 1852, despite all the work done, some stretches of the Washington Canal were impassable.

June. John Maury was elected mayor.

June 11. The Washington Young Men's Christian Association was organized.

August 21. The Balitmore and Ohio Railroad opened a depot on New Jersey Avenue at Northwest C. Street.

November 20. The city council finally allowed Baltimore and Ohio locomotives to run into the city.

1853   The Soldier's Home in the city was opened.

              Congress voted to build a water system for Washington at
              the federal government's expense.

              The Guardian Society of Washington was founded.

              May 28. The city installed gas lamps along all the principal
              thoroughfares and employed a lamplighter to light them.

              June 10. The Georgetown and Catoctin Railroad was char-
              tered, giving the city a spur line connection with the Balti-
              more and Ohio tracks at Point of Rocks, Maryland.

              August 15. Clark Mill's statue of Andrew Jackson was un-
              veiled at Lafayette Square. It was the first equestrian sta-
              tue in the city.

1854   A group of Know-Nothings met at the Washington Monument,
              defaced and threw into the Potomac a block of marble from
              the Temple of Concord in Rome, which the Pope had given
              to the United States for the monument. This incident was
              known as the "Pope-stone episode."

              Building lots in Washington sold for thirty cents a square
              foot.

              March 17. For the first time, street signs went up on lamp-
              posts.

              May 18. An ordinance was passed requiring every building
              in Washington to display its number.

              June. John Tower was elected mayor.

1855   The Government Hospital for the Insane opened in the Dis-
              trict. It came about largely through the work of Dorothea
              Dix of Massachusetts.

              Work stopped on the Washington Monument due to a lack of
              funds.

              By 1855, twelve newspapers, five of them dailies, were pub-
              lished in Washington.

              The Smithsonian Building was finally completed.

March 21. Congress appointed a commission to revise and
codify District law.

December. Railroad tracks were laid from the bridge along
Maryland Avenue to the foot of Capitol Hill, then over First
Street, and across Pennsylvania Avenue to the Baltimore
and Ohio depot. This new road linked the city to Virginia
and was called the Alexandria and Washington Railroad.

December 7. The city council began to lay sewers to drain
surface water into the canal or Potomac River.

1856

A Hebrew congregation was formed by the city's small
Jewish population.

A professional Board of Health was created. Prior to this,
volunteers manned this important city agency.

January. German residents of the city organized a Männer-
chor.

March 3. The city council hired additional scavengers to
help keep the streets clean.

June. William Magruder was elected mayor.

August. Congress spent $2,000 to improve Pennsylvania
Avenue between Capitol Hill and the Treasury.

1857

The Washington Art Association was organized, and held
its first exhibit at the Smithsonian.

February. Congress chartered a school for deaf and dumb
children. It was later merged with the Columbian Institution for the Deaf, Dumb and Blind led by Edward Gallaudet.
The Institution opened in August 1857.

May 27. A spring flood washed away a span of the Long
Bridge.

June 6. A fight broke out at the Northern Liberties Market
polls, causing the Marines to be called out to disperse the
rioters and the polls to be closed.

August 24. The Panic of 1857 hardly touched Washington.
Federal spending, again kept the city solvent.

November 25. The Asylum was destroyed by fire.

1858   Congress moved into its new wing in the Capitol building.

The Senate passed a bill granting Washington $20,000 a year for five years for public school purposes.

February 6. The Washington Seminary changed its name to Gonzaga College and offered an enlarged curriculum.

February 20. Washingtonians defeated a referendum concerning the proposed new legal code for the District.

March. Many members of Congress opposed the tracks of the Alexandria and Washington Railroad running through the city. After a long struggle over the right of way, the Railroad Company collapsed.

April 1. The city council enlarged the police department, but it was still too small to patrol Washington efficiently.

June. James Berret was elected mayor.

December 2. Washington increased the school budget, raised teacher's salaries, and began a night school three evenings a week.

1859   Mayor Berret and the council created a central board which took over most of the functions of the ward overseers of the poor.

By 1859, only 5,800 European immigrants had settled in the city during the previous decade.

January 3. Washington's first water system was completed. It soon proved inadequate for the growing city.

February 28. In Lafayette Square, Congressman Daniel Sickles murdered Philip Barton Key, the son of Francis Scott Key.

October 16-18. Mayor Berret rescinded all the permits he had granted to blacks for the purpose of holding balls and festivals.

1860   Washington's population stood at 61,122, while the total population within the District was 75,080, including 11,000 free blacks.

More than 1,100 children were attending "colored schools" in the District.

Pennsylvania Avenue from the Capitol to the Treasury was paved with cobblestones.

By 1860, the District of Columbia had very few large manufacturing firms.

Only 2,900 pupils, or 29 percent of the white children of school age, were enrolled in the public schools, and illiteracy in the District had risen to eleven percent of the white population.

Washington's first professional baseball team was organized.

February 22. Clark Mill's statue of George Washington was unveiled in Washington Circle.

April 2. St. Ann's Home For Foundlings was opened.

June. Mayor Berret was reelected.

December. Two hundred fifty citizens formed a Washington unit of National Volunteers (Democrats), who anticipated trouble from black Republicans, following Abraham Lincoln's victory in the presidential election.

1861   January. A committee of the House of Representatives investigated an alleged plot by some Washingtonians, sympathetic to the Confederacy, to capture the city. No evidence of a conspiracy was uncovered.

March 4. Abraham Lincoln was inaugurated president. The city remained calm.

March 9. President Lincoln appointed Ward Lamon as Marshal of the District of Columbia.

April. The first District of Columbia volunteers were sworn in at the War Department. Charles P. Stone was appointed Inspector General of these units.

April 12. The firing on Ft. Sumter took place. Fear spread throughout the city that Confederate troops, across the Potomac River, might invade Washington. From this point on, and for the duration of the Civil War, Washington became an armed camp. The city was also crowded with camp followers, furloughed or hospitalized soldiers, and Northern businessmen.

April 25. Regiments of Northern troops began arriving in the city to protect it from Confederate attack. Some Washingtonians left to join Confederate regiments.

June. More than 50,000 volunteers were stationed in and around the city by this date.

July 20-21. The first Battle of Bull Run took place. Congressmen, senators and their wives drove out of the city to watch the battle. With the Union defeat, they hurried back to Washington in panic and became entangled with retreating Union soldiers.

August. President Lincoln ordered work on the Capitol, which had been suspended, resumed.

Two severe fires occurred in the city.

August 6. Congress created a new metropolitan police force, under federal control, for the city.

August 16. Mayor Berret was arrested and jailed as a secessionist because he refused to take the loyalty oath as an official of the new Metropolitan Police Board.

August 27. Mayor Berret resigned after his release from jail. The Board of Aldermen elected Richard Wallach to fill out the mayor's unexpired term.

August 31. Congress ordered all officeholders in Washington to take an oath of allegiance. Some refused, and by the beginning of September, one hundred civilians left government service in the city. More left as the war continued.

September 5. The Washington Hebrew Congregation Synagogue opened.

November 4. The Washington Infirmary on Judiciary Square burned to the ground.

1862   Construction of an extension to the Treasury began.

Northern businessmen began to buy Washington real estate
at high prices. New stores and hotels began to be built.

The Newsboy's Aid was organized.

The Metropolitan Street Railway was organized.

The Washington and Georgetown Street Railroad was chartered. Congress gave it its right of way as a free gift.

The city completed a new market house to replace the old
Centre Market on Pennsylvania Avenue.

January 25. Congress passed a law requiring three month's
schooling yearly for every child in the District between the
ages of six and fourteen, whether white, black, or mixed.

February. A smallpox epidemic struck the city. President
Lincoln himself had a slight case.

March 22. A local Freedman's Relief Association was established to care for the hundreds of slaves now entering
the city. By the Spring of 1863, 10,000 "contrabands" had
gathered in Washington.

April 4. The city council increased the school tax and added
a new tax for building additional schoolhouses.

April 16. The 3,100 slaves owned by District residents
were freed by an Act of Congress.

April 17. The Municipal Black Code in the city was repealed.

May. Congress passed a law requiring Washington voters,
who were challenged at the polls in the city elections,to take
the loyalty oath or lose their votes.

May 10. A law was enacted that required Washington and
the District to open all public schools to black children.

June. Richard Wallach was elected mayor in his own right.

June 3. The city council ruled that public school teachers
must take the oath of loyalty.

July. Congress broadened the duties of the Metropolitan Police to include sanitary inspections and abatement of nuisances. Ten police inspectors were assigned to the new Sanitary Corps.

1863   The police made 24,000 arrests in the city, which was three and a half times the number of arrests made in Brooklyn, a city with a population twice that of the entire District.

A congressionally financed aqueduct was completed in Washington, providing pure water for the residents.

The dome of the Capitol was completed.

A reorganized judiciary was provided for the District.

Congress appropriated money to light the streets in the city that were most essential for transportation.

January 1. Following President Lincoln's Emancipation Proclamation, thousands of black people entered the city.

February 25. As a result of the National Banking Act, the First National Bank opened in Washington with a capitalization of $500,000.

March 10. The War Department began helping with sanitation and garbage collection in the city.

March 17. Secretary of War, Edmund M. Stanton, established a "colored home" in the house of Richard Coxe of Georgetown.

May. The federal government opened a "contraband village" on the outskirts of the city. Three thousand blacks from Washington moved there.

July. City garbage carts began making regular rounds.

December 3. Thomas Crawford's statue "Freedom" was placed on top of the new Capitol dome.

1864   Congress doubled the pay of policemen in the city to $2.62 a day. There were still only 88 men on the force.

February 11. The city council set up a salaried fire department and bought it equipment.

March. The trustees of the black schools in the city opened the first black public school in the Ebenezer Church.

March 18. Vaccination of every child in Washington was made compulsory. Children in the public schools were vaccinated.

April 30. Congress agreed to share the cost of work on streets with the city, but no federal funds were provided.

June. Arlington National Cemetery, on part of Robert E. Lee's plantation across the Potomac River from Washington, was dedicated.

June 6. Mayor Wallach was reelected.

July 4. The new Wallach School, with ten classrooms, was opened.

July 11. General Jubal Early's Confederate cavalry raided the District of Columbia, but were driven off.

1865 By 1865 there were only a few black public schools in the District. The city council provided very little money for them.

The Washington Board of Trade was organized.

Congress chartered the Metropolitan Branch of the Baltimore and Ohio Railroad.

February. A fire destroyed most of the Indian paintings hanging at the Smithsonian Gallery.

March. The Bank of the Metropolis became the National Metropolitan Bank of Washington.

March 4. For the first time, blacks in the city took part in the inaugural parade.

April 9. Robert E. Lee surrendered to Ulysses S. Grant at Appomattox Court House. By the end of the war, the District of Columbia provided the Union Army with 13,265 white men and 3,260 blacks.

April 14. John Wilkes Booth shot Abraham Lincoln as he was sitting in a box at Ford's Theater in Washington.

December 18. Voters in the District defeated a referendum providing for black suffrage in the District of Columbia.

WASHINGTON COMES OF AGE - 1866-1899

1866   The white population of the city stood at 70,000 people.

Between 1866 and 1867 Washington's black population increased 12 percent, and they owned one-fifth of all privately held real estate in the city.

Row houses were built in the area east of the Capitol.

The Columbia Hospital for Women and Lying-in Asylum opened.

The House of Correction for Boys opened.

June. Mayor Wallach was elected for a fourth term.

July. Empty army barracks in the District were used as schoolrooms for blacks. Congress appropriated $10,000 for building schoolhouses for black children.

December. President Andrew Johnson's proposal to give the District representation in Congress was defeated.

December 16. An act providing for unrestricted manhood suffrage in the District of Columbia was passed by Congress. Some District residents were opposed.

1867   Howard University was chartered. It was originally biracial.

The Industrial Home School was founded.

A new YMCA and a Masonic Temple were constructed.

June. Blacks in Washington elected their first black councilman.

October 25. Construction began on a new building for the Department of Agriculture.

1868   The Balitmore and Potomac Railroad began building a road to enter the city. In 1870 it received right of way from Congress.

April. Washingtonians dedicated their memorial to Abraham Lincoln.

May 1. Washington's twenty year city charter expired. It was renewed until the District committees of Congress could develop an alternative document.

June 3. Sayles J. Bower was elected mayor. Two blacks, John F. Cook and Carter Stewart, were elected to the city council.

October. The city council appropriated $34,000 for the black schools in Washington.

1869   The National University was founded.

Washingtonians pledged $2,000,000 to finance a world's fair in the city. Congress refused to allow it to be held there. Philadelphia was selected as the site of the first American world's fair.

February. Congress merged the white and black school boards in the city.

June. Six black councilmen and one black alderman were elected.

June 10. The city council passed a civil rights law. It fined any owner of any place of public entertainment who refused accomodations to blacks.

September. The first mixed school in the city was established. The plan was abandoned a year later, and separate schools for white and black continued in Washington.

1870   Washington's population reached 109,199, while that of the District stood at 131,700.

Only about one-third of all black children of school age were attending any type of school in Washington.

The Washington Market Company was chartered.

March 7. The city council passed another civil rights law. It forbade discrimination towards blacks in restaurants, bars, hotels, and other places of amusement.

April 14. The first black newspaper in the city, the New Era, was published. Its editors were Frederick Douglas and Sella Martin.

June. By June 1870, fifteen miles of sidewalks and four miles of sewers had been constructed. Two hundred miles of streets were still unpaved.

June 16. Matthew Emery was elected mayor.

October. The repaving of Pennsylvania Avenue began.

November 22. Mayor Emery began the construction of the first adequate sanitary sewage system in the city.

1871   The Washington Philosophical Society was founded with Joseph Henry as its president. Simon Newcomb, Salmon P. Chase, Ainsworth Spofford, Lester Frank Ward, Francis A. Walker and others were members.

Tiber Creek, near the White House, was drained and filled in. Up to that time, it was an open sewer.

February 21. Congress passed the District Territorial Act ending municipal government in Washington and the District of Columbia. The city and the District would now be governed by a governor and council appointed by the president. Only a lower house would be elected. A District delegate would sit in Congress, but had no vote. All municipal functions would be handled by appointed boards.

March. Congress authorized a multi-million dollar building for the State, War, and Navy Departments.

April 14. President Ulysses S. Grant appointed Henry D. Cooke Governor of the Territory of the District of Columbia.

April 19. Norton Chipman was elected the Territory's non-voting delegate to Congress.

May-June. The Territorial Legislature created 400 appointive jobs to handle the duties formerly carried out by 160 city and District officials.

June 10. The new Board of Public Works proposed a multi-million dollar plan for public improvements in the city.

They included new sewers, better paved streets, beautification programs, and the like. The driving force behind
the plan was Alexander Shepherd.

September. By the fall of 1871 Alexander Shepherd became
the political boss of Washington and leader of the so-called
District Ring.

1872   January. Congress began a long investigation into the affairs of the District.

May. Congress commended Alexander Shepherd and the
Board of Public Works for their service to the District. The
congressional investigation, begun in January, turned up no
wrongdoing.

July-August. Washington was hit by a serious smallpox epidemic.

December 19. The Territorial Legislature passed another
District Civil Rights Law to safeguard the rights of blacks.

1873   The first Civil War memorial in the city, a statue of General John A. Rawlins, was placed on Pennsylvania Avenue
at Ninth Street.

Stewart Castle was constructed near Dupont Circle.

July. Vaccination for all District residents was made compulsory.

September 18. When the Panic of 1873 struck, Washington
went bankrupt. It was already tottering because of Shepherd's manipulations. Banks closed and unemployment
mounted.

September 24. President Grant appointed Alexander Shepherd governor of the District of Columbia after Henry D.
Cooke resigned the post.

October 14. A white normal school was opened in the city.
A few months later, the school was made biracial.

1874   Henry Kirk Brown's statue of General Winfield Scott was unveiled in Scott Circle.

The city signed a contract with the Odorless Excavating Apparatus Company, which introduced suction pumps and airtight containers to take away the contents of the city's privies.

The official Revised Statutes of the District of Columbia appeared. It codified the local laws existing since 1801.

The Board of Health condemned 389 unsanitary buildings, the first such action ever taken in the city.

The Washington Literary Society was founded.

January 1. The city's indebtedness was $19,000,000.

February. A second congressional investigation of the affairs of the District opened. The committee again found no wrongdoing.

June. Congress abolished the governorship, the legislature, and the board of public works, and temporarily placed control of the District in the hands of three commissioners appointed by the president. A committee was appointed to draft a bill for a permanent form of government. William Dennison of Ohio was appointed the head of the commission.

June 7. The first black Roman Catholic church in Washington, St. Augustine's, was constructed.

June 15. A House Judiciary Committee recommended that the federal government pay 50 percent of the annual costs of running the District.

December. A new Reform School for Boys opened; it was a segregated institution.

1875   July. A reduction in the number of District jobs, followed by a cut in laborers' wages, caused severe problems for a number of Washingtonians.

1876   Radicals on the central Republican committee of the District of Columbia drafted a platform which condemned separate black and white schools. Nothing came of it.

February 25. Congress appropriated $25,000 for relief purposes as the city was still feeling the effects of the Panic of 1873.

November 22. President Grant ordered 450 army regulars to the city, in the wake of the disputed election of 1876.

1877   As late as 1877 Washington still contained 56,000 cesspools and vaults.

September 15. Thomas B. Bryan, a newly appointed District commissioner, called a citizens meeting to discuss the formation of a labor exchange.

1878   The Cosmos Club was organized at the home of John Wesley Powell.

More than 400,000 square yards of asphalt were laid on the streets of Washington in an attempt to solve the city's paving problem.

Some 300 Washington businessmen obtained from Congress a charter for a National Fair Association.

After 1878 the various Civil Rights Acts were repeatedly violated and segregation and discrimination prevailed.

The first telephone wires of the Chesapeake and Potomac Telephone Company were strung on the city's streets.

March 29. Congress appropriated $15,000 for draining and filling the swamps south of the Capitol.

June. Congress passed the Organic Act, by which Washingtonians lost all self-government. The administration of the city was placed in the hands of three permanent commissioners appointed by the president. The federal government promised to meet half the District's annual budget. This form of government continued until 1961 when Washington was finally given a municipal charter once again.

August. The Potomac River flooded areas in the lower part of the city.

1879   A new all black high school was opened with private funds.

August 22. Isadore Saks opened a clothing store in the city.

1880   Washington's total population was 197,000 people, 140,000 white, and the rest black or mulatto.

1881   In 1881, less than a third of the 30,474 houses in the city
               had sewer connections.

               August. The first white high school in the city was opened.

1882   Congress appropriated funds for the filling of the tidal
               marshes. A tidal basin was built downstream in order to
               control the flow of the tide.

               The Garfield Hospital was chartered.

               January 5. Electric arc lights were installed on some of
               the major streets of the city. All wires, however, were
               laid underground.

               April. Washington established its branch of the Associated
               Charities.

               April 12. The Georgetown Amateur Orchestra was founded.

1884   Congress appropriated funds for the laying of additional wa-
               ter mains and sewers.

               A Young Women's Christian Association was established in
               the city.

               December 6. The Washington Monument, 555 feet high, was
               finally completed. It was dedicated on February 22, 1885.

1885   William Bramwell Powell was appointed superintendent of
               the city's white schools. Before his dismissal in 1900, he
               made Washington's school system one of the best in the coun-
               try.

1886   The Washington Music Club was founded.

               A Home for Friendless Colored Girls was opened, but due
               to a lack of money it closed within a few months.

               April. A new dam was built at the Great Falls to facilitate
               a better water supply for the city. Poor construction at the
               connecting tunnels caused cave-ins, and only a complete re-
               building of the aqueduct several years later made this sys-
               tem operative.

               May 1. Washington's labor unions condemned the violence
               of the Haymarket Riot in Chicago.

1887   Washington's population reached 250,000 people.

                During this year, 2,450 buildings were constructed in Wash-
                ington, and land was selling at 48 cents a square foot.

                March. The Guardian League was organized.

                May. The Washington Athletic Club was opened.

                September. A real estate syndicate purchased Chevy Chase,
                the old Joseph Bradley farm. It became Washington's first
                country club.

1888   By 1888 a Washington metropolitan area was developing, and
                Congress enacted a law requiring suburban developers to
                make their communities conform to the street plan of the
                city.

                The Corcoran School of Art was founded with a gift of
                $100,000 left by William W. Corcoran upon his death.

                May. Congress rejected a proposal made by Theodore
                Noyes for a constitutional amendment enabling qualified vo-
                ters in the District to elect representatives to Congress and
                the Electoral College.

1889   A flood damaged the Chesapeake and Ohio Canal so badly
                that canal traffic stopped completely for the next seven or
                eight years.

                November. Catholic University of America opened in Wash-
                ington.

                November 1. The new Washington Board of Trade was
                founded with Beriah Wilkens as its first president.

                November 12. The Gridiron Club was founded by Washing-
                ton's newspaper correspondents.

1890   Washington's population numbered 255,000 people. Blacks
                constituted 33 percent of the total, a proportion larger than
                in any other big city of the nation at this time.

                By 1890 there were 23,000 government employees living in
                Washington; by 1901, the total ran to over 26,000.

Washington had 181 electric arc lights, and added 75 to 100 more yearly thereafter.

John Ross, a college professor, was appointed a District commissioner.

February. The building trades unions went out on strike, but failed to win improvements.

April 19. Congress created a Superintendent of Charities to supervise all public charity agencies in the city. Amos G. Warner was appointed to the post.

June 1. The District Appropriations Act included $200,000 for the establishment of a National Zoological Park north of the city. The driving force behind the zoo was Samuel Langley, Secretary of the Smithsonian Institution.

August. John Philip Sousa played his Washington Post March for the first time, at the Smithsonian Institution.

1891   Henry Adams' memorial to his wife was unveiled at Rock Creek Cemetery. The statue was done by Augustus St. Gaudens.

1892   The commissioners opened a Municipal Lodging House and Wood Yard for vagabonds and tramps.

Congress established the Board of Children's Guardians. William Redin Woodward was appointed head of the Board.

January. Telephone connections were established between Washington and Boston, and Washington and New York.

February 20. A health measure was adopted by the commissioners. It prohibited the building of dwellings in alleys less than twenty feet wide and not equipped with sewage, water main connections and lights.

June 21. The Democratic National Party platform included a District home rule plank.

1893   The Cathedral Foundation was organized and granted a charter by Congress. Charles Glover was its founder.

A Highway Act was passed by Congress for Washington and its surrounding suburbs.

May 5. The Panic of 1893 stopped building construction in the city. There was unemployment and want, but the city did not experience as widespread suffering as other large cities. Government spending again helped.

July. A cholera epidemic struck the city. Less deaths occurred than in any previous epidemic year.

November. A School for Incorrigible Girls was opened.

1894   The National Cathedral School for Girls opened. It was founded by the Cathedral Foundation.

A new law completely revised real estate assessments.

A new building code prevented the construction of houses without plumbing.

March 25-August 1. The "army of the unemployed," led by Jacob Coxey, came to Washington to ask the federal government for help. Camps were set up in the city.

June. The Commissioners enforced Sunday closing laws. They increased fines for the illegal sale of liquor and reduced the number of liquor licenses granted.

1895   February 11. The city of Georgetown was incorporated into Washington and became a fashionable section of the greater city.

April. Rudolph Henning, a sanitary engineer, helped plan a new sewage and water disposal system.

1897   Trinity College for women was opened.

The Sanitary Improvement Company was established. It developed low cost, clean housing.

February. The Library of Congress moved from the Capitol to a new building that cost more than $6,000,000. It became the largest library in the world.

March. The modern Corcoran Gallery of Art was opened on Seventeenth Street.

March 4. Twenty black women organized the Treble Clef Club.

September. A law passed by the commissioners ordered all houses in the city to be connected to sewers.

1898   Construction began on the new sewage disposal system.

American University was opened by the Methodists, but the college was not used for the next nineteen years.

January. The Washington Academy of Sciences was founded with Gardiner Hubbard as its first president.

The Sanitary Improvement Company built a number of houses for workingmen and extended the trolley lines into the area.

August. Kindergartens were first opened in Washington.

1899   The police force was increased to 585 men, and a new bicycle squad was added to the department.

Work began on an extension to the reservoir.

May. A Height of Buildings Act was passed, limiting private construction to fourteen stories.

October. The Home for Incurables was established.

WASHINGTON IN THE TWENTIETH CENTURY
1900-1940

1900   The total population of the city was 278,718, including 90,000 black residents.

By 1900 four out of every five native American whites in the District of Columbia had been born in the South.

The development of the "Great White City" in Chicago, prompted the "City Beautiful" movement in Washington. Congress began to investigate plans for the city's improvement.

By 1900 Washington was the best paved city in the world. A variety of paving materials were used, but asphalt was the most successful method.

April. A Congressional Act reorganized the Washington School system. A seven member Board of Education was created and the school budget was increased considerably.

June. The thirteen independent city trolley car lines were
merged to become the Washington Traction and Electric
Company.

1901   An advisory commission for the improvement and beautification of greater Washington was appointed.

The District of Columbia had all of its laws codified.

By 1901 the new sewage disposal system was almost half
completed.

Centralized financial control was established for all of Washington's charitable institutions.

February. Congress passed two bills giving favored treatment to the Pennsylvania and Baltimore and Ohio Railroads
within city limits.

March 1. Under Senator James McMillan a commission was
appointed to plan a complete park system for the city. By
June 1, 1901, the Park Commission submitted a list of recommendations.

December. Washington celebrated its centennial, which was
tied in with the beautification movement and the creation of
the park system. Such architects as Daniel Burnham, Charles
McKim, and Frederick L. Olmsted Jr., were hired as consultants.

1902   The Carnegie Institution was founded in Washington on a gift
of $10,000,000 from Andrew Carnegie.

January. The Park Commission submitted its first official
report. Its recommendations called for extensive changes
in the entire layout of the city.

April. The Washington Symphony Orchestra was founded
by Reginald Dekoven. It disbanded during the fall of 1902.

April 14. The Committee on the Improvement of Housing
Conditions was organized by the District commissioners.
Charles Weller was appointed chairman. Members included
George Kober, Henry Satterlee, and S.W. Woodward.

1903   The District Public Library (now the Martin Luther King

Memorial Library) was built on Mt. Vernon Place. Andrew Carnegie gave the money for its construction.

The American Civic Association was founded in Washington. It was the leading advocate of the beautification movement for the city.

1904   George Kober and George Sternberg founded the Sanitary Housing Company. Its purpose was to build inexpensive housing for alley dwelling families.

1905   The present day system of naming streets in Washington was adopted.

1906   Congress created a board with authority to condemn unsanitary buildings in the city.

April. An organized black protest to Washington's Jim Crow laws took shape. These campaigns for equal rights were led by such important blacks in the city as Kerry Miller, Calvin Chase, Mary Church Terell, and George W. Cook.

1907   The pumping station, sewage disposal plant, and water filtration system for the District were completed.

February. The new Union Railroad Station was completed.

May 6. The Washington Chamber of Commerce was developed as an offshoot of the Board of Trade.

October. The Panic of 1907 had little effect upon the banking or building operations of the District, again, as a result of government activity.

1908   The Washington Tuberculosis Hospital was opened.

By 1908 the District Building, the new offices for the House of Representatives and the Senate, and the new Department of Agriculture Building were completed.

June. The Lion Bridge spanning Rock Creek Valley was constructed.

October. The Women's Congressional Club was founded in the city.

1909   The District of Columbia Excise Board was established.

September 22. Congress passed a law which required the District commissioners to submit their annual budgets as statements of expected revenues from District taxes and matching federal funds.

1910   The population of the city stood at 278,718, of which 97,186 were black residents.

Congress created a permanent Fine Arts Commission. It was an advisory board for fine arts projects undertaken in the city.

As a result of suburban development, by 1910, the areas surrounding Washington contained a quarter of the District's total population.

March. A law was passed allowing the height of buildings in the city to rise twenty to fifty feet higher than the law of 1899 had allowed.

April 1. The new National Museum opened.

May. Continental Hall, built by the Daughters of the American Revolution, was opened.

1911   The Children's Council was organized in the city. It attempted to stop the spread of juvenile delinquency.

January. A new workhouse was opened at Occoquan.

April. Japanese cherry trees were planted along the Tidal Basin. By 1915 they were in bloom.

May 26. The Federation of Citizen's Associations was formed.

1912   Lorado Taft's Columbus Memorial Fountain was unveiled.

Griffith Stadium, for the Washington Nationals professional baseball team, was opened.

May. A branch of the National Association for the Advancement of Colored People was formed in the city. Within a few months it was one of the largest in the country.

1913   Washington's population rose to more than 333,000 people.

                A city directory for blacks was published for the first time
                in Washington. It was never published again.

                President Woodrow Wilson appointed Frederick Siddons a
                District Commissioner.

                January 1. A series of segregationist rules, in all the fed-
                eral departments in Washington, went into effect.

                February 15. An all black Y.M.C.A. was opened.

                May. The Washington Neighborhood House Auxiliary was
                organized to do kindergarten work in the slums.

1914   June 28. World War I broke out in Europe. A large percen-
                tage of Washingtonians believed that the United States should
                remain neutral.

                July 2. Congress passed the so-called "red light" bill,
                which closed up all the houses of prostitution in the city.
                Many illegal houses continued to operate.

                September. The Washington Junior League was founded.

                October. Congress passed the Alley-Dwelling Act, which
                was designed to convert the worst alleys in the city into
                streets or parks. The Act also prohibited the construction
                of any type of housing in certain narrow alleys. Mrs. Wood-
                row Wilson was the driving force behind the passage of this
                important statute.

1916   The Department of the Interior Building was erected.

                By 1916, next to government business and real estate, the
                tourist trade was Washington's leading financial resource.

                October. The all black battalion of the District of Columbia
                National Guard was sent to the Mexican border. Segrega-
                tion also prevailed in the armed forces of the city.

                November 15. The Lorton Reformatory was opened.

                November 23. Because of the work of B. Pickman Mann,
                the Children's Protective Association was formed.

1917   The Gallinger Hospital, Washington's first municipal hospital, was completed and opened.

April 6. The United States' Declaration of War against Germany saw most District residents take their patriotism seriously and participate in a variety of war activities.

May-June. Resolutions presented in the House and Senate for a Constitutional Amendment to give the District of Columbia voting representation in Congress and the Electoral College were defeated.

August. Women suffragists picketed the White House, causing riots and disorders. District Commissioner Louis Brownlow ordered the arrest of several of the leading pickets, all of them prominent Washingtonians.

1918   More than 17,000 Washingtonians served in the armed forces during World War I.

January 1. A serious housing shortage existed in the Capital, as a result of the influx of war workers of all kinds.

May 25. Congress passed a resolution to prevent rent profiteering in the city, which had developed as a result of the housing shortage.

September 21. An epidemic of Spanish influenza struck the city, but only a few residents died of the disease.

November 11. Throughout the war years the city became a national war center. People poured into Washington. The city's population increased from 350,000 in 1914 to more than 526,000 by the end of 1918. The facilities of the District were seriously overtaxed.

December. The demand for housing rose, as many of the wartime residents of the city remained.

1919   January. A citizen's committee again asked Congress for the enfranchisement of District residents. Again no action was taken by Congress.

January 18. Commissioner Brownlow established an all black platoon in the fire department.

July 19-23. Five days of rioting and street fighting took place in the city, caused by racial hatred and the panic that developed when a bomb was found in the house of Attorney General A. Mitchell Palmer.

December. Congress cut the Federal share of District appropriations to 40 percent instead of the former 50 percent. A new fiscal act was passed for the city.

1920   Congress enacted a District minimum wage law for women.

A group of Washingtonians established Community Services, with the purpose of opening nonsegregated neighborhood centers.

January. By the beginning of 1920 it was clear that Washington had become a big city.

March 20. A controversy developed over the refusal of the Board of Education to reappoint the Superintendent of Schools, and over the retention of Assistant Superintendent Roscoe Conkling Bruce. The Negro Parents League demanded his removal.

May. The Senate refused to confirm President Wilson's nominee, John Van Schaick, as Superintendent of Schools.

June. Commissioner Brownlow appointed an interracial committee of citizens to develop means of improving communications between whites and blacks in Washington.

September 1. Louis Brownlow resigned to become city manager of Petersburg, Virginia. His loss was a serious blow to the District government. Mabel Boardman was appointed to fill the vacancy.

September 20. The Washington Council of Social Workers was founded.

1921   The Washington Catholic Charities was established.

March 4. Warren G. Harding was inaugurated, and an era of calm settled over the city.

June. A business slump caused some unemployment. Congress cut District appropriations as well.

November 11. The Unknown Soldier was placed in Arlington National Cemetery.

1922   By 1922 the ratio of black to white inhabitants in the city had dropped. It continued to decline throughout the decade. Southern blacks began migrating to the Northern urban industrial centers rather than to Washington.

May 30. The Lincoln Memorial, with Gutzon Borglum's statue of Lincoln, was completed and dedicated.

October. Business revival occurred in Washington. New private building projects began.

1923   The District Building Code was revised by the Board of Trade. An advisory council of the American Institute of Architects helped plan the new code.

The District Public School Association was organized.

1924   Construction began on a new Potomac River bridge to run from the Lincoln Memorial to the Arlington Cemetery.

The Washington Chamber Music Society was founded.

July. Congress created the National Capital Park Commission. It had authority to acquire land for parks, parkways, and playgrounds in the District. It was also given the responsibility for the planning of Metropolitan Washington.

September 1. A new school attendance law was adopted requiring all children between the ages of 6 and 16, black and white, to attend the public schools.

September 21. The Washington Senators professional baseball team won the World Series.

1925   Robert S. Brookings built an office building to provide revenue for his center for economic research.

The United States Chamber of Commerce Building was constructed.

Congress increased the size of the police force, began a five year school building program, enlarged the water supply, and began to extend the sewage system.

January. Congress authorized the five year building program at an estimated cost of $20,185,000.

February. Congress fixed the federal contribution to yearly District expenses at $9,000,000.

July. More than 25,000 members of the Ku Klux Klan paraded down Pennsylvania Avenue.

October. The Coolidge Auditorium was completed.

1926 A single Board of Public Welfare was created for the District by Congress. The new board was headed by George S. Wilson. Other members were John Jay Edson and Coralie Cook.

More than $50,000,000 worth of federal building acitivities were begun in the city.

January 8. The District Supreme Court upheld the legality of housing discrimination. Blacks could not purchase houses in white neighborhoods.

1927 The new Brookings Institute was established.

Congress cut the federal share in District appropriations still further.

April. The first Cherry Blossom Festival was held in the city. It became an annual affair.

October 17. Congress passed a Mother's Pension Act for the District of Columbia.

December. Buildings for the Department of Commerce and the Bureau of Internal Revenue began to be constructed.

1928 The Friends of Music, located in the Library of Congress and headed by Nicholas Longworth, was founded.

April. Congress passed a District Workmen's Compensation Act.

May 1. The first Community Chest Drive in Washington was conducted.

1929 June. Workmen began to remove the World War I dormitories from Union Station Plaza, to construct a new Municipal Center, to relocate the Botanic Garden, to construct an Arboretum, to erect a new Department of Agriculture Building, and to select a site for a Supreme Court Building facing the Capitol.

June 14. A new published code of laws for the District of Columbia appeared.

October. Washington was not hit as badly as other cities by the stock market crash and the ensuing nationwide depression. Federal spending and activity once again came to the city's rescue.

1930   A building program for the construction of the Federal Triangle was begun.

Motor vehicle registrations stood at 173,600 and parking in the city had become a serious problem, compounded by a lack of public parking spaces and garages.

Gallinger Hospital was completed. It provided Washington with a fine municipal hospital.

January. Frederic A. Delano became chairman of the National Capital Park Commission; and under him, progress was made in beautifying the city.

June 1. President Herbert Hoover appointed a new set of District Commissioners; they were Luther H. Reichelderfer, Herbert B. Crosby, and John C. Gotwals.

1931   February. Congress authorized an $8,000;000 District public works program of street paving, sewer and bridge construction, and the extension of the water mains to the suburbs.

October 11. The National Symphony Orchestra was created in Washington through private subscriptions.

December. About a thousand unemployed men from different areas of the country came to Washington to hold a demonstration for federal aid.

1932   The Arlington Memorial Bridge across the Potomac River to the National Cemetery was opened.

Elder Lightfoot Michaux established his Church of God in the District.

June. Thousands of World War I veterans staged the famous Bonus March, demanding the immediate cashing of adjusted compensation certificates in full. By late June the Bonus Army reached 17,000 veterans, many of whom camped on the Anacostia Flats at the edge of the city.

July 1. For the first time, Washington was seriously affected by the depression. Federal jobs and salaries were cut, businesses went bankrupt, and lifetime savings were wiped out.

July 28-29. When Congress refused to take any real action in behalf of the unemployed veterans, most of them left the city. However, about 2,000 of them refused to depart. An attempt by the Washington police to force them to go caused the death of two of the veterans and two of the policemen. President Hoover called out federal troops to remove the veterans. The action of the troops, commanded by General Douglas MacArthur, was extremely harsh.

December 15. Constitution Avenue was christened.

1933   By 1933 the depression became worse in Washington. Teachers' salaries were cut, but, interestingly enough more new schoolhouses were provided than in any one previous year.

January. The Folger Shakespeare Library opened.

March 3. Congress adjourned without voting any District appropriations for 1934.

March 4. Franklin D. Roosevelt was inaugurated president. Washingtonians felt that he would obtain for them full voting rights and provide relief for the city.

March 14. Banking resumed in the District of Columbia after the Bank Holiday ten days earlier. Washington was the first city in the nation to resume full banking operations.

July 1. President Roosevelt cut more than 17,000 residents of the city off the pension rolls as part of his Economy Act.

August 1. The Welfare Board began administering unemployment relief for Washington, but by December its funds were used up.

September. The Washington Senators professional baseball team won the American League pennant.

October. In order to check discriminatory employment practices in the city, a group of men formed the New Negro Alliance whose purpose was to organize black consumers in the struggle for equal rights. This group, through boycotts and other devices, was partially successful.

November 5. The Metropolitan Police Boys Club was organized.

November 16. President Roosevelt appointed Melvin D. Hazen and George E. Allen District commissioners.

1934

An Alley Dwelling Authority was created to clean up the worst slum sections of the city.

Public nursery schools were opened in Washington.

January. At the beginning of 1934 almost 200,000 people were out of work in the city.

July. By the summer a measure of prosperity had returned to the city. The tourist trade began to pick up once more.

1935

Greenbelt, Maryland, a planned Washington suburb, was laid out under the auspices of the Resettlement Administration headed by Rexford Tugwell. Other suburban communities also began to develop.

Construction began on a new sewage treatment plant for the city.

March. The federal bureaucracy in Washington grew during Roosevelt's New Deal years. By the spring of 1935 there were 93,000 government employees living in and around Washington.

October. All streetcar and bus companies were merged into a single system, the Washington Transit System.

1936   Congress attached the so-called Red-Rider clause to the
                School Appropriation Act of 1936, which denied salary to
                any Washington teacher who taught the principles of Com-
                munism in his classroom. The rider was dropped in 1939.

1937   The National Gallery of Art, a gift of Andrew Mellon, be-
                gan to be constructed.

                The Supreme Court Building, as well as the Federal Triangle,
                and the second House Office Building were completed. In
                addition, the Department of the Interior Building, the Police
                Court, and the Bureau of Printing and Engraving were al-
                most completed.

                The Federal Writers Project WPA Guide to Washington was
                published.

                The new Department of Agriculture Building was erected
                and dedicated.

                July. Construction began on the Municipal Center.

                November. The Graduate School of American University
                began to admit black students.

1938   There were 9,717 blacks in federal service in Washington.
                Ninety percent of them, however, held custodial jobs.

                The Budapest String Quartet became a resident quartet in
                Washington.

                April 30. In a city referendum, Washingtonians voted on
                two question concerning home rule and enfranchisement.
                Those who voted, overwhelmingly favored their own city gov-
                ernment in the District, as well as representation in Con-
                gress and the Electoral College. Nothing came of this vote,
                as Congress refused to act on any bills which would change
                the government of the District.

                December. The Washington Urban League was chartered.

1939   April. The Library of Congress Annex was completed.

                April 13. Construction on the Jefferson Memorial was be-
                gun.

April 25. After having been refused permission to give a concert in the DAR owned Constitution Hall, the famous black singer, Marian Anderson, gave the concert at the Lincoln Memorial. More than 75,000 people attended. This event is usually considered the turning point in Washington blacks' fight against discrimination.

October. Archibald MacLeish was appointed Librarian of Congress.

1940

Washington's total population stood at 663,000 people. By 1940, 55,000 additional blacks had migrated to Washington during the previous decade. More than 30,000 of them had come from the South. The ratio of black to white, which had declined during the 1920s, was reversed.

January. By 1940, civil service employment in Washington was 129,000.

June. The construction of 3,000 public housing units in the city was completed.

August. Federal employment in the city rose to 166,000.

October. Beginning in October, as a result of the outbreak of World War II in Europe, numbers of administrative and clerical personnel came to Washington, causing housing and office shortages. This situation would be characteristic of the city during World War II.

November. At the convention of the Congress of Industrial Organization, delegates representing 4,000,000 workers, unanimously endorsed suffrage for the District of Columbia.

WORLD CAPITAL - 1941-1970

1941

January 4. Franklin D. Roosevelt was inaugurated at the White House; the only inaugural conducted at that building.

February. By late winter all semi-skilled and skilled workmen in the city had found jobs. For the next four and a half years, unemployment was not a problem in the District of Columbia.

March 24. The National Gallery was opened to the public.

April. A District Council of Defense was created. It set up committees of volunteers to coordinate private and government activities in the city.

June. Congressional hearings on the question of home rule for the District took place. Again no action was taken by Congress.

August. The District of Columbia National Airport was opened.

November. The so-called dollar-a-year men began arriving in Washington to work on the defense effort.

December 7. The Japanese attacked Pearl Harbor. Washingtonians, like the rest of America, were angry at this action.

December 31. By the end of the year Washington's population rose to 750,000 people.

1942   Japanese cherry trees were planted along the tidal basin where the Jefferson Memorial was under construction.

January 1. Rent controls went into effect in Washington.

April. The Jefferson Memorial, begun in 1939, was completed and dedicated.

May. The District Recreation Board was formed. Its program of activities contained no racial restrictions.

August. Tire, gasoline, and automobile rationing caused Washingtonians to use bicycles on the streets. Commuting to the suburbs was made difficult.

1943   The Pentagon was completed and opened for immediate occupancy.

June. A Washington Citizen's Committee on Race Relations was organized.

December. New hearings were held on a new bill for the reorganization of the District of Columbia's government, but home rule would have to wait until the war was over.

1944   Nearly 600 well-to-do black families moved into Mayfair
                Mansions, a middle-class housing project developed by El-
                der Lightfoot Michaux.

1945   April 14. President Roosevelt's funeral procession passed
                Constitution Avenue en route to the White House.

                May. A Redevelopment Act for Washington was passed by
                Congress. It gave the National Capital Park and Planning
                Commission authority to plan the rebuilding of all of the
                city's slum areas, to lay out a new highway system, and to
                choose sites for the construction of new public buildings.
                Ulysses S. Grant III was appointed the commission chair-
                man.

                May 8. V-E Day was celebrated in the city. Compared to
                several of the other big urban centers, Washington was quiet.

                August 14. A large crowd gathered in Lafayette Square to
                hear the announcement of the Japanese surrender.

                September-Ocotber. Demobilization of the civilian work
                force in Washington took place. Large numbers of people
                began to leave the city, but not as many as had been antici-
                pated. As a result, Washington experienced another popu-
                lation increase.

1946   November. A national committee of prominent Americans
                was formed to fight segregation in Washington.

                November 6. A public referendum was again held in Wash-
                ington on the question of home rule. Again, Washingtonians
                voted for local self-government, though not as overwhelm-
                ingly as in 1938.

1947   A biracial Washington Home Rule Committee was organized.

                July. A series of Joint House and Senate Subcommittee
                hearings on District Governmental Reorganization took place.
                No action was forthcoming.

1948   Construction of the Dupont Circle underpass was begun.

                February. A poll conducted by the Washington Post revealed
                that seventy percent of those who answered wanted a change
                in the city's government.

May. A new Home Rule Bill for the District of Columbia was sponsored by Congressman James Auchincloss of New Jersey. Congress shelved it.

1949   The Strayer Report on Washington's public school system was made public. Written by George Strayer of Columbia University, the report stressed the inequalities in the education offered whites and blacks in the city. It also criticized the inadequacies of physical accomodations, and the shortcomings in teacher recruitment and promotion among other things.

1950   Washington's population reached 813,000 people.

The Planning Commission's first published report since 1932 presented a series of proposals for the improvement of Washington's physical and human environment.

The 1950 census showed that of the 3,887 residential blocks in Washington, nonwhite residences had spread into 459 more than in 1940, and the number of exclusively white blocks had dropped from 2,041 to 1,956.

Civil service jobs in Washington were fewer than they had been in any year during the 1940s.

In 1950 the NAACP persuaded the District commissioners to hold a hearing at which blacks presented a bill of particulars against the Washington Chief of Police.

The Washington Conference of Christians and Jews started a workshop on human relations for some of the Metropolitan Police.

July 27. All the public swimming pools in the District were desegregated.

1951   The remodeling of the White House, begun in 1949, was completed.

A massive program of slum clearance in Southwest Washington began. A number of restaurants, schools, shopping centers, town houses, low rental houses, expensive apartment buildings, and government office buildings were constructed during the next few years.

To preserve the historic character of Georgetown, Congress forbade architectural changes, unless approved by the Fine Arts Commission.

June. Rent controls in Washington were ended.

1952   Congress enacted a measure which granted new authority to the District commissioners to make a number of minor appointments for the District without the approval of the president.

June. Judge David Pine of the District Court ordered the admission of deaf black children in the District of Columbia to the Kendall Green school in Washington.

1953   June 15. The United States Supreme Court upheld the validity of the Equal Services Acts, passed in the District in the 1870s, forbidding racial discrimination in restaurants and other places of public entertainment.

August. All movie houses and theaters in the city were integrated.

1954   May 17. The Supreme Court, in the case of Brown v. the Board of Education of Topeka, Kansas, handed down its famous school desegregation order.

September 1. For the first time in the city's history, racially integrated schools opened in Washington.

1955   A National Capital Regional Planning Council was appointed to develop an intelligent plan for land use in the district.

September. School desegregation in the District was completed.

1957   A Joint Congressional Committee on Washington Metropolitan Problems was created and a thorough study of the problems of the District of Columbia was undertaken. During the following year the committee made a number of important recommendations, the most important of which was the creation of a Regional Development Agency to be given the authority to develop a comprehensive master plan for the Standard Metropolitan Washington Area.

April. Carl Hansen, an ardent believer in desegregated public schooling, was appointed superintendent of schools.

1958   The Washington Hospital Center was completed.

              Almost total reconstruction of an additional   550 acres of
              Washington's slums was begun under the authority of the
              District of Columbia Redevelopment Land Agency.

              Wesley Theological Seminary opened.

              December. Sanitary experts discovered that some water
              mains were being used for sewage and the drainage of sur-
              face water. Construction of a new sewage and water drain-
              age system began during the following year to remedy this
              defect.

1959   Construction began on the Capital Beltway, a circumferen-
              tial highway to encircle the metropolitan area, and an in-
              ner loop to expedite traffic in the heart of the city.

              The new Senate Office Building was completed.

              March. The Adams-Morgan Project, in a run-down 42 block
              biracial neighborhood, was completed with funds obtained
              from the Housing and Home Finance Agency.

              April 14. The Taft Memorial, in memory of Senator Robert
              A. Taft of Ohio, was constructed on the Capitol grounds and
              dedicated.

              June. District Commissioner Robert McLaughlin forbade
              uniformed Washington policemen to solicit funds for the
              Metropolitan Police Boy's Club unless the club was integrated.
              By 1962 these clubs were all integrated.

1960   The population of Washington was 763,956, some 50,000
              less than ten years earlier. The city had lost 36.8 percent
              of its population largely to its surrounding suburbs. How-
              ever, the Standard Metropolitan Area of Washington con-
              tained a population of 2,001,897 people.

              The total number of blacks living in the District of Columbia
              accounted for 53.9 percent of its total population.

              The East Front of the Capitol was extended and faced with
              marble.

              By 1960 there were fifty research and development compan-
              ies located in Washington.

1961   The District of Columbia Stadium, renamed in 1969 the
                Robert F. Kennedy Memorial Stadium, was completed.

                The Woodrow Wilson and George Mason Bridges across the
                Potomac were constructed.

                The Arena Stage Theater, a theater in the round, was opened.
                Its productions became nationally recognized.

                The Library of Congress held 39,000,000 items in its col-
                lections.

                February. The K Street Expressway, under Washington
                Circle, was completed and dedicated.

                April 3. The Twenty-Third Amendment to the Constitution,
                giving residents of the District of Columbia the right to vote
                for president and vice-president, was ratified.

1962   The Theodore Roosevelt Island Bridge across the Potomac
                was constructed.

                The District of Columbia's Fair Housing Ordinance was
                passed.

                Congress established the Washington Metropolitan Area
                Transit Authority to coordinate and control all public trans-
                portation and highways within the city's Standard Metropoli-
                tan Area.

1963   Dulles International Airport was completed and opened.

                August 28. Martin Luther King, Jr. led a massive March
                on Washington to protest racial inequalities. More than
                100,000 people from all over the nation gathered at the Lin-
                coln Memorial to hear King deliver his "I have a dream"
                speech.

1965   The Smithsonian's new History and Technology Building was
                constructed.

                The new House Office Building, named for former Speaker
                of the House Sam Rayburn, was ready for occupancy.

                The Washington Metropolitan Council of Governments was
                created to harmonize the policies of Washington and the sub-
                urban jurisdictions.

July-August. Minor incidents of rioting occurred in Washington during the summer of 1965 as blacks demanded a greater degree of civil rights.

1966   The redevelopment of Pennsylvania Avenue began.

1967   Loudoun and Prince William Counties, Virginia, were added to the Washington Standard Metropolitan Area.

The Reorganization Plan for the District of Columbia, sponsored by President Lyndon Johnson, was adopted by Congress. The District commissioners were to be replaced by a presidentially appointed mayor, deputy mayor, and nine-man bipartisan council. The council was to be biracial in composition.

The Most Reverend Patrick A. O'Boyle, Catholic Archbishop of Washington, was designated a Cardinal by Pope Paul IV.

Federal City College was founded, and Frank Farmer was named its president.

November 1. Washington's commission form of government went out of existence. President Johnson appointed Walter E. Washington, a black, as the first mayor of the city under the new plan, while John W. Hechinger was named the first chairman of the new city council.

December. Patrick V. Murphy was appointed Director of Public Safety, a new post, to replace the old position of Chief of Police. In addition a twenty-one point crime control program was instituted for the District.

1968   The first District of Columbia Model Cities Commission was elected by District voters.

A Community Facilities Center was opened.

April 4-6. A wave of rioting spread through Washington in the wake of the assassination of Martin Luther King, Jr. President Johnson ordered out federal troops to deal with the rioters. Considerable damage was done to various parts of the city, but no loss of life occurred.

May. A "poor people's march" on Washington took place as blacks, Chicanos, and poor whites from every part of the

country piled into the city to protest the government's attitude toward poverty, welfare and related issues.

May-June. A poor people's encampment, known as Resur-
rection City was set up in Washington under the leadership
of the Reverend Ralph Abernathy. Shantytowns and tents
went up on the malls and in the parks, causing serious problems of health, sanitation, and water supply.

November 4. An elective Board of Education was provided
for Washington. It was the first in the city's history.

1969   January. President Richard Nixon reappointed Walter Washington as mayor and named Thomas W. Fletcher as deputy
mayor.

April 28. President Nixon proposed a series of steps to improve the District's government, including a Constitutional
Amendment that would provide the District with one or more
voting members in the United States House of Representatives and possibly two senators.

June. Considerable sentiment was expressed by many Washingtonians in favor of separate statehood. No official action
was taken.

November 15. More than 250,000 persons paraded down
Pennsylvania Avenue in a massive peaceful appeal for a
speedy withdrawal of United States troops from Vietnam.

December 9. Formal groundbreaking for the District's rapid rail transit system took place.

1970   The population of the city declined still further to 746,169,
but the total population of the Standard Metropolitan Area
increased to 2,835,737.

The John F. Kennedy Memorial Center for the Performing
Arts was dedicated.

Residents and interns at D.C. General Hospital walked out
for seventeen hours as a result of a salary dispute.

The proposal to give the District representatives in the
House, passed by the Senate in 1969, received final approval.

No action was taken on President Nixon's proposal to create a fifteen member commission to write a self-government charter for the city.

Congress refused to appropriate the city's $35,000,000 share for the Metropolitan Subway construction. A loan of $57,000,000 from the Federal Department of Transportation kept construction on schedule.

Increased efforts were made to resolve Washington's chronic problems in education, crime, social services, and revenues.

President Nixon appointed Graham W. Watt as the city's second deputy mayor.

March. The city's Department of Human Resources, headed by Philip J. Rutledge, was created.

May. The D.C. Crime Bill was passed by Congress, and was to go into effect on February 1, 1971.

May 9. More than 100,000 antiwar demonstrators gathered in Washington to protest United States involvement in Vietnam.

July 1. The Board of Education adopted the "Clark Plan," proposed by psychologist Kenneth B. Clark, which called for paying Washington teachers' salaries partly on the basis of how much their students improved during each year. The teachers' union vehemently protested this action.

October. Hugh J. Scott, a black, was appointed Superintendent of Schools; the first black to serve in this position.

December 31. As 1970 came to an end, Washingtonians looked forward to voting for their representative to Congress during the following year and to continued improvements in self-government, race relations, education, crime control and transportation.

DOCUMENTS

The documents found on the following pages have been carefully selected to provide the reader with as wide a spectrum of the facets of Washington's history as possible in a book of this kind. Obviously, much more could have been included, but the limitations of space precluded the author from expanding the documents section of this work. Nevertheless, the excerpts presented here give the reader a good picture of the physical, demographic, economic, and political changes that have taken place during the more than one hundred and eighty years of Washington's existence.

Documentary materials concerned with the nation's capital are relatively easy to obtain, since most of the important papers fall within the public domain and can be found in any library housing a relatively good collection of Congressional records, debates, transcriptions and newspapers. For the more localized materials, the Library of Congress and the Washingtoniana Division of the Martin Luther King Memorial Library in Washington D.C. are indispensable. The latter contains a very complete collection of all the primary documents relating to the city's governmental, economic and socio-cultural developments, while the former includes these materials within its collection, as well as all the official Senate, House and Executive documents pertaining to the capital. In addition, the Library of Congress Manuscript Division and the National Archives house many unpublished sources, such as official papers, personal papers and letters, and records of business organizations and social agencies. These, too, provide the student with valuable primary material necessary for research on Washington.

THE RESIDENCE ACT -- 1790

In July, 1790, Congress passed the Residence Act allowing President George Washington to choose two sites for the National Capital along a stretch of the Potomac River. The following selection is this act.

Source: William A. Davis, ed., The Acts of Congress in Relation to the District of Columbia from July 16th, 1790, to March 4th, 1831, Washington, D.C., 1831.

AN ACT for establishing the temporary and permanent Seat of the Government of the United States.

Sec. 1. Be it enacted by the Senate and House of Representatives of the United States of America in Congress assembled, That a district of territory, not exceeding ten miles square, to be located as hereafter directed, on the river Potomac, at some place between the mouths of the Eastern Branch and Connogocheague, be, and the same is hereby accepted for the permanent seat of the government of the United States: Provided, nevertheless, That the operation of the laws of the state within such district shall not be affected by this acceptance, until the time fixed for the removal of the government thereto, and until Congress shall otherwise by law provide.

Sec. 2. And be it further enacted, That the President of the United States be authorized to appoint, and by supplying vacancies happening from refusals to act, or other causes, to keep in appointment, as long as may be necessary, three commissioners, who, or any two of whom, shall, under the direction of the President, survey, and, by proper metes and bounds, define and limit a district of territory, under the limitations above mentioned; and the district so defined, limited, and located shall be deemed the district accepted by this act, for the permanent Seat of the Government of the United States.

Sec. 3. And be it enacted, That the said commissioners, or any two of them, shall have power to purchase or accept such quantity of land on the eastern side of the said river, within the said district, as the President shall deem proper, for the use of the United States, and according to such plans as the President shall approve; the said commissioners, or any two of them, shall, prior to the first Monday in December, in the year one thousand eight hundred, provide suitable buildings for the accommodation of Congress, and of the President, and for the Public offices of the government of the United States.

Sec. 4. And be it enacted, That, for defraying the expense of such purchases and buildings, the President of the United States be authorized and requested to accept grants of money. . . . .

AMENDMENT OF THE RESIDENCE ACT -- 1791

On March 3, 1791, Congress amended the Residence Act, enlarging the boundaries of the District of Columbia, and prohibiting the construction of public buildings on the Virginia side of the Potomac River.

Source: William A. Davis, ed., The Acts of Congress in Relation to the District of Columbia from July 16th, 1790, to March 4th, 1831, Washington, D.C., 1831.

AN ACT to amend "An Act for establishing the temporary and permanent Seat of the Government of the United States.*

Be it enacted by the Senate and House of Representatives of the United States of America in Congress assembled, That so much of the act, entitled "An act for establishing the temporary and permanent Seat of the Government of the United States," as requires that the whole of the district of territory, not exceeding ten miles square, to be located on the river Potomac, for the permanent Seat of the Government of the United States, shall be located above the mouth of the Eastern Branch, be, and is hereby repealed; and that it shall be lawful for the President to make any part of the Territory below the said limit, and above the mouth of Hunting Creek, a part of the said district, so as to include a convenient part of the Eastern Branch, and of the lands lying on the lower side thereof, and also the town of Alexandria; and the territory so to be included, shall form a part of the district not exceeding ten miles square, for the permanent Seat of the Government of the United States, in like manner and to all intents and purposes, as if the same has been within the purview of the above recited act; Provided, That nothing herein contained shall authorize the erection of the public buildings otherwise than on the Maryland side of the river Potomac, as required by the aforesaid act.

Approved, March the 3d, 1791.

WASHINGTON'S FIRST CHARTER -- 1802

Although the city has been established in 1790, it did not receive its first charter of incorporation until twelve years later. What follows is part of the Act of 1802.

Source: District of Columbia Code, 1967 Edition, vol. I, Washington, D.C.,
1967.

An ACT To incorporate the inhabitants of the city of Washington, in the
District of Columbia

Be it enacted by the Senate and House of Representatives of the
United States of America in Congress assembled, That the inhabitants
of the city of Washington be constituted a body politic and corporate,
by the name of a mayor and council of the city of Washington, and by
their corporate name, may sue and be sued, implead and be impleaded,
grant, receive, and do all other acts as natural persons, and may purchase and hold real, personal and mixed property, or dispose of the
same for the benefit of the said city; and may have and use a city seal,
which may be broken or altered at pleasure; the city of Washington
shall be divided into three divisions or wards, as now divided by the
levy court for the county, for the purpose of assessment; but the number may be increased hereafter, as in the wisdom of the city council
shall seem most conducive to the general interest and convenience.
     Sec. 2. And be it further enacted, That the council of the city of
Washington shall consist of twelve members, residents of the city,
and upwards of twenty-five years of age, to be divided into two chambers,
the first chamber to consist of seven members, and the second chamber
of five members; the second chamber to be chosen from the whole number of councillors elected, by their joint ballot. The city council to be
elected annually, by ballot, in a general ticket, by the free white male
inhabitants of full age, who have resided twelve months in the city,
and paid taxes therein the year preceding the election being held: the
justices of the county of Washington, resident in the city, or any three
of them, to preside as judges of election, with such associates as the
council may, from time to time, appoint.
     Sec. 3. And be it further enacted, That the first election of members
for the city council shall be held on the first Monday in June next, and
in every year afterwards, at such place in each ward as the judges of
the election may prescribe.
     Sec. 4. And be it further enacted, That the polls shall be kept
open from eight o'clock in the morning till seven o'clock in the evening,
and no longer, for the reception of ballots. On the closing of the poll,
the judges shall close and seal their ballot-boxes, and meet on the
day following in the presence of the marshal of the district, on the
first election, and the council afterwards, when the seals shall be

broken, and the votes counted: within three days after such election, they shall give notice to the persons having the greatest number of legal votes, that they are duly elected, and shall make their return to the mayor of the city.

Sec. 5. And be it further enacted, That the mayor of the city shall be appointed, annually, by the President of the United States. He must be a citizen of the United States, and a resident of the city, prior to his appointment.

Sec. 6. And be it further enacted, That the city council shall hold their sessions in the city hall, or, until such building is erected, in such place as the mayor may provide for that purpose, on the second Monday in June, in every year; but the mayor may convene them oftener, if the public good require their deliberations. Three fourths of the members of each council may be a quorum to do business, but a smaller number may adjourn from day to day: they may compel the attendance of absent members, in such manner, and under such penalties, as they may by ordinance, provide: they shall appoint their respective presidents, who shall preside during their sessions, and shall vote on all questions where there is an equal division; they shall settle their rules of proceedings, appoint their own officers, regulate their respective fees, and remove them at pleasure: they shall judge of the elections, returns and qualifications of their own members, and may, with the concurrence of three fourths of the whole, expel any member for disorderly behaviour, or mal-conduct in office, but not a second time for the same offence: they shall keep a journal of their proceedings, and enter the yeas and nays on any question, resolve or ordinance, at the request of any member, and their deliberations shall be public. The mayor shall appoint to all offices under the corporation. All ordinances or acts passed by the city council shall be sent to the mayor, for his approbation, and when approved by him, shall them be obligatory as such. But if the said mayor shall not approve of such ordinance or act, he shall return the same within five days, with his reasons in writing therefor; and if three fourths of both branches of the city council, on reconsideration thereof, approve of the same, it shall be in force in like manner as if he has approved it, unless the city council, by their adjournment, prevent its return.

Sec. 7. And be it further enacted, That the corporation aforesaid shall have full power and authority to pass all by-laws and ordinances; to prevent and remove nuisances; to prevent the introduction of contagious diseases within the city; to establish night watches or patrols, and erect lamps; to regulate the stationing, anchorage, and mooring of vessels; to provide for licensing and regulating auctions, retailers of liquors, hackney carriages, wagons, carts and drays, and pawnbrokers within the city; to restrain or prohibit gambling, and to provide for licensing, regulating or restraining theatrical or other public amusements within the city; to regulate and establish markets; to erect and repair bridges; to keep in repair all necessary streets, avenues, drains and sewers, and to pass regulations necessary for the preservation of the same, agreeably to the plan of the said city . . . .

THE AMENDED CHARTER OF THE CITY -- 1804

In 1804, Washington's charter was amended to make both chambers of its council elective. The council was also given additional powers, and schools were provided for.

Source: William A. Davis, ed., The Acts of Congress in Relation to the District of Columbia. . . ., Washington, D.C., 1831.

Be it enacted by the Senate and House of Representatives of the United States of America in Congress assembled, That the act, entitled ''An act to incorporate the inhabitants of the city of Washington, in the District of Columbia, except so much of the same as is inconsistent with the provisions of this act, be and the same is hereby continued in force for and during the term of fifteen years from the end of the next session of Congress.

Sec. 2. And be it further enacted, That the council of the city of Washington, from and after the period for which the members of the present council have been elected, shall consist of two chambers, each of which shall be composed of nine members, to be chosen by distinct ballots, according to the directions of the act to which this is a supplement; a majority of each chamber shall constitute a quorum to do business; in case vacancies shall occur in the council, the chamber in which the same may happen, shall supply the same by an election, by ballot, from the three persons next highest on the list to those elected at the preceding election; and a majority of the whole number of the chamber in which such vacancy may happen, shall be necessary to make an election.

Sec. 3. And be it further enacted, That the council shall have power to establish and regulate the inspection of flour, tobacco, and salted provisions; the guaging of casks and liquors; the storage of gun powder, and all naval and military stores, not the property of the United States; to regulate the weight and quality of bread; to tax and license hawkers and pedlars; to restrain or prohibit tipling houses, lotteries, and all kinds of gaming; to superintend the health of the city, to preserve the navigation of the Potomac and Anacostia rivers, adjoining the city; to erect, repair, and regulate public wharves, and to deepen docks and basins; to provide for the establishment and superintendence of public schools; to license and regulate exclusively, hackney coaches, ordinary keepers, retailers and ferries; to provide for the appointment of inspectors, constables and such other officers as may be necessary to execute the laws of the corporation; and to give such compensation to the mayor of the city as they may deem fit.

Sec. 4. And be it further enacted, That the levy court of the county of Washington shall not hereafter possess the power of imposing any tax on the inhabitants of the city of Washington.

APPROVED, February 24, 1804.

WASHINGTON'S BLACK CODE -- 1808

In December 1808, the Washington City Council enacted the city's first Black Code. It resulted from pressure applied by the Southern-born residents of the city, who formed the majority of the population. By Southern standards, however, the code was moderate. A portion of this code follows.

Source: Samuel Burch, ed., A Digest of the Laws of the Corporation of the City of Washington, to the first of June, 1823 . . ., Washington, D.C., 1823.

. . . . 23. That if any slave be convicted under any of these provisions, the owner or owners of such slave shall be liable for the same, and judgement may be rendered against such owner or owners, by any justice of the peace as aforesaid, upon the conviction of the slave, but it shall be optional with the owner or owners of such slave or slaves, to have the whole of the fine remitted, except fifty cents, on condition he, she or they give directions to have the offending slave whipt, according to the judgment of the magistrate, who is hereby directed to remit so much there of, the residue to go to the person who inflicts the punishment. (Act 6th December, 1808.)

24. That it shall be duty of each constable, when called on by any of the citizens of their respective wards to attend and disperse or take into custody any slave or person of colour, if offending against the laws of the city or county of Washington, and if taken, to have him or them carried before any one of the justices of the peace for the county of Washington, to be dealt with according to law. (Act 6th December, 1808, and 31st May, 1811.)

25. That it shall not be lawful for any person to entertain a slave or slaves after ten o'clock P.M. and for every slave found in the house or dwelling of another, after ten o'clock P.M. the person so entertaining them, shall forfeit and pay five dollars, but no fine shall be recovered of any person in whose house such slave or slaves are found, if it should appear they were sent there on any message by their master or mistress. (Act 6th December, 1808.) . . . .

THE SECOND CHARTER -- 1812

Washington received a new charter from Congress, which vested the choice of the mayor in the hands of a new twenty man council elected by the voters. Part of this charter follows.

Source: <u>District of Columbia Code</u>, 1967 Edition, vol. I, Washington, D.C., 1967.

AN ACT Further to amend the charter of the city of Washington

Be it enacted by the Senate and House of Representatives of the United States of America in Congress assembled, That from and after the first Monday of June next, the corporation of the city of Washington shall be composed of a mayor, a board of aldermen and a board of common council, to be elected by ballot, as herein after common council, to be elected by ballot, as herein after directed. The board of aldermen shall consist of eight members, to be elected for two years, two to be residents of and chosen from each ward by the qualified voters resident therein; and the board of common council shall consist of twelve members, to be elected for one year, three to be residents of and chosen from each ward in manner aforesaid: and each board shall meet at the council chamber on the second Monday in June next (for the despatch of business) at ten o'clock in the morning, and on the same day and at the same hour annually thereafter. A majority of each board shall be necessary to form a quorum to do business, but a less number may adjourn from day to day, The board of aldermen, immediately after they shall have assembled in consequence of the first election shall divide themselves by lot into two classes; the seats of the first class shall be vacated at the expiration of one year, and the seats of the second class shall be vacated at the expiration of two years, so that one half may be chosen every year. Each board shall appoint its own president from among its own members, who shall preside during the sessions of the board, and shall have a casting vote on all questions where there is an equal division: Provided, such equality shall not have been occasioned by his previous vote.

Sec. 2. And be it further enacted, That no person shall be eligible to a seat in the board of aldermen or board of common council, unless he shall be more than twenty-five years of age, a free white male citizen of the United States and shall have been a resident of the city of Washington one whole year next preceding the day of election, and shall at the time of his election, be a resident of the ward for which he shall be elected, and possessed of a freehold estate in the said city of Washington, and shall have been assessed two months preceding the day of election. And every free white male citizen of lawful age, who shall have resided in the city of Washington for the space of one year next preceding the day of election, and shall be a resident of the ward in which he shall offer to vote, and who shall have been assessed on the books of the corporation not less than two months prior to the day of election, shall be qualified to vote for members to serve in the said board of aldermen and board of common council, and no other person whatever shall exercise the right of suffrage at such election.

Sec. 3. And be it further enacted, That the present mayor of the city of Washington shall be, and continue such until the second Monday in June next, on which day, and on the second Monday in June annually thereafter, the mayor of the said city shall be elected by ballot of the board of aldermen and board of common council in joint meeting, and a majority of the votes of all the members of both boards shall be necessary to a choice; and if there should be an equality of votes between two persons, after the third ballot, the two boards shall determine the choice by lot. He shall, before he enters upon the duties of his office, take an oath or affirmation, in the presence of both boards, "lawfully to execute the duties of his office to the best of his skill and judgment, without favour or partiality." He shall exofficio, have and exercise all the powers, authority and jurisdiction of a justice of the peace for the county of Washington, within the said county. He shall nominate, and, with the consent of a majority of the members of the board of aldermen, appoint to all offices under the corporation, (except the commissioners of election,) and any such officer shall be removed from office on the concurrent remonstrance of a majority of the two boards. He shall see that the laws of the corporation be duly executed, and shall report the negligence or misconduct of any officer to the two boards. He shall appoint proper persons to fill up all vacancies during the recess of the board of aldermen, to hold such appointment until the end of the then ensuing session. He shall have power to convene the two boards, when in his opinion the good of the community may require it; and he shall lay before them from time to time, in writing, such alterations in the laws of the corporation, as he shall deem necessary or proper, and shall receive for his services annually, a just and reasonable compensation, to be allowed and fixed by the two boards, which shall neither be increased nor diminished during the period for which he shall have been elected. Any person shall be eligible to the office of mayor, who is a free white male citizen of the United States, who shall have attained to the age of thirty years, and who shall be the bona fide owner of a freehold estate in the said city, and shall have been resident in the said city two years immediately preceding his election: and no other person shall be eligible to the said office. In case of the refusal of any person to accept the office of mayor upon his election thereto, or of his death, resignation, inability or removal from the city, the said two boards shall elect another in his place to serve the remainder of the year . . . .

A MORE STRINGENT BLACK CODE -- 1812

As the black population of Washington increased, alarmed white
residents called for a toughening of the Black Code that had
been passed four years earlier. What follows is a portion of
the new Black Code passed by the City Council in response to
these demands.

Source: Samuel Burch, ed., A Digest of the Laws of the Corporation
of the City of Washington, to the First of June, 1823 . . ., Washington,
D.C. 1823.

. . . . 17. That it shall not be lawful for slaves to assemble in
any house, street, or other place, by day or by night, in a disorderly
or tumultuous manner, so as to disturb the peace or repose of the
citizens; the slave or slaves so offending shall be taken up by any
constable, within whose knowledge the fact may come, or may be taken
up by any other citizen, seeing hearing, or knowing of it, and carried
before a justice of the peace, and, on conviction, shall be sentenced to
receive any number of stripes on his, or her bare back not exceeding
twenty. (Act 16th December, 1812.)
       18. That if any free black or mulatto person, or slave, shall be
found playing cards, dice, or other game, of an immoral tendency,
whether for money or other thing, or not, or shall be present as one
of the company where such game is playing, such free black or mulatto
person, on the fact being made appear to a justice of the peace as aforesaid, shall pay a fine of ten dollars; and if the offender by unable or
refuse to pay the same, he, or she, shall be confined to labor for a
time not exceeding thirty days, for each offence, or if the offender be
a slave, he or she shall be punished with any number of lashes on their
bare back, not exceeding fifteen. (Act 16th December, 1812.)
       21. That if any slave shall have a dance, ball, or assembly, at
his, her or their house, without first obtaining a permit for that purpose from the mayor, he, she or they, shall each pay a fine of twenty
dollars, or be sentenced to confinement and labor for a time not exceeding thirty days; in case of inability or refusal to pay such fine for
each offence, he, she or they shall each receive any number of lashes
on their bare back, not exceeding ten; and the mayor after being con-
vinced of the safety and propriety of the solicited permission, shall
therein state the number of guests to which the assembly is to be
limited, and the hour at which it shall be broken up; and if a greater
number shall be found attending, or if the company shall not be broken
up at the appointed time, the person to whom the permit shall have
been granted, shall, on conviction, pay a fine not exceeding ten dollars;
and in case of inability or refusal to pay the same, shall be confined
to labor for a time not exceeding ninety days; or shall receive on his
or her bare back a number of lashes not exceeding ten. (Act 16th December, 1812.)

22. That no slave or free black or mulatto person, shall be allowed to go at large through the streets, or other parts of the said city, at a later hour than ten o'clock at night, from the first day of April to the first day of October; or than nine o'clock at night, from the first day of October, to the first day of April; and that it shall be the duty of the constables, and lawful for any free white citizen to apprehend and take before some justice of the peace, any or all such persons as may be found so going at large, except such slave be furnished with a written permission from his master, mistress or employer; or such free black or mulatto have a pass from a justice of the peace, or from some other crediable citizen, or be engaged in driving a cart, waggon, dray or other carriage. A slave offending against this section of the law, shall be punished at the discretion of the justice of the peace, before whom he or she may be taken, with a number of stripes on his or her bare back not exceeding thirty-nine; and the free black or mulatto, shall, on conviction, be fined in a sum not exceeding twenty dollars; on refusal or inability to pay such fine, he, she or they shall be sentenced to confinement at labor not exceeding ninety days: (Act 16th December, 1812.)

26. That the commissioners of the corporation be charged with the execution of the act of 16th December, 1812, and the constables are required to be vigilent in the discharge of the duties of their office; for any failure or neglect to do which, they shall, on conviction, be fined a sum not exceeding ten, nor less than five dollars. (Act 16th December, 1812.)

THE THIRD CHARTER OF WASHINGTON -- 1820

Washington received a new charter from Congress with enlarged powers in all municipal affairs. The most important new provision concerned the right of the citizenry to elect their Mayor.

Source: District of Columbia Code, 1967 Edition, vol. I, Washington, D.C., 1967.

AN ACT To incorporate the inhabitants of the city of Washington, and to repeal all acts heretofore passed for that purpose

Be it enacted by the Senate and House of Representatives of the United States of America, in Congress assembled, That the act, entitled "An act to incorporate the inhabitants of the city of Washington, in the District of Columbia," and the act supplementary to the same, passed on the twenty-fourth of February, in the year one thousand eight hundred and four, and the act, entitled "An act further to amend the charter of the city of Washington," and all other acts, or parts of acts, inconsistent with the provisions of this act, be, and the same are hereby, repealed: Provided, however, That the mayor, the members of the board of aldermen, and the members of the board of common council, of the corporation of the said city, shall and may remain and continue as such, for and during the terms for which they have been respectively appointed, subject to the terms and conditions in such cases legally made and provided; and all acts or things done, or which may be done, by them in pursuance of the provisions, or by virtue of the authority, of the said acts, or either of them, and not inconsistent with the provisions of this act, shall be valid, and of as full force and effect as if the said acts had not been repealed.

Sec. 2. And be it further enacted, That the inhabitants of the city of Washington shall continue to be a body politic and corporate, by the name of the "Mayor, board of aldermen, and board of common council, of the city of Washington," to be elected by ballot, as hereinafter directed, and, by their corporate name, may sue and be sued, implead and be impleaded, grant, receive, and do all other acts, as natural persons; and may purchase and hold real, personal, and mixed, property, or dispose of the same, for the benefit of the city; and may have and use a city seal, and break and alter the same at pleasure.

Sec. 3. And be it further enacted, That the mayor of the said city shall be elected on the first Monday in June next, and on the same day in every second year thereafter, at the same time and place, in the same manner, and by the persons qualified to vote for members of the board of aldermen and the board of common council. That the commissioners hereinafter mentioned shall make out duplicate certificates of the result of the election of mayor; and shall return one to the board of aldermen and the other to the board of common council, on the Monday next ensuing the election; and the person having the greatest number of votes shall be the mayor: but in case two or more persons, highest in vote, shall have an equal number of votes, then it shall be lawful for the board of aldermen and the board of common council to proceed forthwith, by ballot, in joint meeting, to determine the choice between such persons. The mayor shall, on the Monday next ensuing his election, before he enters on the duties of his office, in the presence of the boards of aldermen and common council, in joint meeting, take an oath, to be administered by a justice of the peace, "lawfully to execute the duties of his office, to the best of his skill and judgment, without favour or partiality." He shall, ex officio, have and exercise all the powers, authority and jurisdiction, of a justice of the peace for the county of Washington, within the said county. He shall nominate, and with the consent of the board of aldermen, appoint to all offices under the corporation, (except commissioners of election,) and may remove any such officer from office at his will and pleasure. He shall appoint persons to fill up all vacancies which may occur during the recess of the board of aldermen, to hold such appointments until the end of the then ensuing session. He may convene the two boards when, in his opinion, the public good may require it; and he shall lay before them, from time to time, in writing, such alterations in the laws of the corporation as he may deem necessary and proper; and he shall receive, for his services, annually a just and reasonable compensation, to be allowed and fixed by the two boards, which shall neither be increased nor diminished during his continuance in office. Any person shall be eligible to the office of mayor who shall have attained to the age of thirty years, who shall have resided in the said city for two years immediately preceding his election, and who shall be the bona fide owner of a freehold estate in the said city; and no other person shall be eligible to the said office. In case of the refusal of any person to accept the office of mayor, upon his election thereto, or of his death, resignation, inability, or removal from the city, the said boards shall assemble and elect another in his place, to serve for the remainder of the term, or during such inability.

Sec. 4. And be it further enacted, That the board of aldermen shall consist of two members to be residents in, and chosen from, each ward, by the qualified voters therein, and to be elected for two years, from the Monday next ensuing their election: and the board of common council shall consist of three members, to be residents in, and chosen from, each ward, by the qualified voters therein, and to be elected for one year, from the Monday next ensuing their election; . . . .

A CONTEMPORARY DESCRIPTION OF WASHINGTON
1826

The following selection is a fairly accurate and
amiable description of the Nation's Capital in
1826, written by a female resident of the city,
who was an outstanding author of travel books.

Source: Anne Royall, Sketches of History, Life and Manners in the United
States, New Haven, 1826.

. . . It was not long before the towering dome of the capitol met my
eye: its massy columns and walls of glittering white. The next object that
strikes the eye of a stranger, is the President's house, on the left, while
the capitol is on the right, as you advance in an eastern direction. Another
object of admiration is the bridge over the Potomac. The capitol, however,
which may aptly be called the eighth wonder of the world, eclipses the whole.
This stupendous fabric, when seen at a distance, is remarkable for its magnitude, its vast dome rising out of the centre, and its exquisite whiteness.
The President's house like the capitol, rivals the snow in whiteness. It is
easily distinguished from the surrounding edifices, inasmuch as they are of
brick. Their red walls and black, elevated roofs, form a striking contrast
to the former, which is not only much larger, but perfectly white, and flat
on the top. From the point just mentioned, it has the appearance of a quad-
rangular; it displays its gorgeous columns at all points, looking down upon
the neighboring buildings in silent and stately grandeur. The War Office,
Navy Office, the Treasury department, the Department of State, the General Post Office, and the City Hall are all enormous edifices. These edifices;
the elevated site of the city; its undulating surface, partially covered with
very handsome buildings; the majestic Potomac, with its ponderous bridge,
and gliding sails; the eastern branch with its lordly ships; swelling hills
which surround the city; the spacious squares and streets, and avenues,
adorned with rows of flourishing trees, and all this visible at once; it is not
in the power of imagination to conceive a scene so replete with every species of beauty. . . .

THE SOUTHARD REPORT
1835

In February 1835 Samuel Southard delivered a report to Congress, which, among other things, stated
that the national capital was the concern of the entire country, and that federal spending in and for
the city was justified.

Source: The Southard Report, Doc. 97, 23C, 2nd S, 268 ser., February
2, 1835.

That the well known pecuniary embarrassments of the city, and the re-
peated appeals which have been heretofore made to the justice and liberal-
ity of Congress, have induced a diligent and careful examination into the
facts and principles which are applicable to the case.

Those embarrassments are of the most painful description. The city
is involved in pecuniary obligations from which it is utterly impossible that
it can be relieved by any means within its own control, or by any exertions
which it may make, unaided by Congressional legislation. Its actual debts
now amount to the enormous sum of $1, 806, 442 $\frac{59}{100}$; and it has not means
from which it can apply at this time a single dollar for its discharge. So
perfectly exhausted have its resources become, that it will, very probably
in a short time, be driven to the surrender of its charter, by neglecting to
elect its corporate officers, and thus be left upon the hands of Congress to
dispose of, govern, and sustain as may best suit their own views of what is
proper for the capital of the Union. That the Senate may see the items
which compose the amount of the city debts, the committee append a statement (A) by which they are exhibited. A part of the engagements of the city,
in relation to the stock which it holds in the Chesapeake and Ohio canal, it
is known to Congress are of a kind which must be promptly satisfied, or
the property of the inhabitants exposed to sale in a few months under the
orders of the Executive of the United States; and its creditors, who are foreign bankers, in all probability will become the owners of a great proportion of the property within the capital of the Union. A state of things so
little creditable to the nation, and so abhorrent to the feelings of the committee that they will not hesitate to recommend such measures, within the
constitutional authority of Congress, as, in their judgment, are called for
by the occasion.

The committee deem it proper, in the first place, to state that, in the
investigation of the causes which have led to the embarrassed condition of
the city, they have not found reason to rebuke and condemn the imprudence
or extravagance of the inhabitants and the city authorities to the extent which
they had anticipated. They have, it is believed, in some instances been mis-

led into expenditures which did not appropriately belong to them, but the
views by which they were governed were of a liberal and public spirited
character. Such has been the fact in relation to the streets. They have
also contracted engagements in regard to the Chesapeake and Ohio canal
into which it was imprudent for them to enter; but they erred with others,
and find countenance in the opinions and recommendations of the Government and of public men, with whom it is no reproach to be associated in
opinion and action. The committee do not find in their conduct any thing
which should excite in Congress a reluctance to come to their relief. The
first cause of embarrassment to which the attention of the committee was
directed was the expense incurred in the opening and repairs of the streets.
The plan of the city is one of unusual magnitude and extent. The avenues
and streets are very wide, and for the number of the inhabitants much
greater in distance than those of any other city on this continent; and necessarily require a proportionate expenditure to make and keep them in repair.
And as the city has not grown in the usual manner, but has necessarily been
created in a short space of time, the pressure for the public improvements
has been alike sudden and burdensome. The population is but little more
than twenty thousand, of whom near seven thousand are people of color and
slaves; and a large number are temporary residents, connected with the
Governement. The avenues vary from one hundred and twenty to one hundred and sixty feet in width; the streets from eighty to one hundred and forty-
seven; the average being about ninety feet. The avenues and streets which
have to be opened and repaired, to fill up the plan of the city, embrace a
distance of more than sixty miles. Upon the streets, then, has been expended since the year one thousand eight hundred, an average annual sum
of not less than $13,000, exclusive of a nearly equal amount assessed upon
the inhabitants, for the pavements, gutters, &c.; a sum enormous in its
amount, when the character and resources of the population, and their scattered position, and the other improvements which they have been compelled
to make are considered. While this burden from the streets was upon them,
and within the short period since the city was founded, they have been compelled to create their market-houses, infirmaries, pumps, wells, lamps,
fire engines and houses; pay their proportion for county roads; and the expenses of their police, &c.

The expenditure upon the streets, under these circumstances, has un-
questionably been one of the principal causes of the embarrassment of the
city; and the committee believe that it is one which ought not to have been
thrown on the inhabitants to the extent which it has been. They found this
opinion upon the early history of the city, the object of the nation in its establishment, and the contracts made by the Government for the land which
it possesses within its limits. . . .

THE SMITHSONIAN INSTITUTION
1846

In 1846, by congressional act, the world-famous
Smithsonian Institution was established. The Institution's activities embrace all branches of science and social science relating to the United States.
The following selection is a portion of the act creating one of the world's truly unique cultural and
scientific centers.

Source: Smithsonian Institution, The Smithsonian Institution: Documents
Relative to Its Origin and History, Washington, D.C., 1901.

An act to establish the "Smithsonian Institution," for the increase and diffusion of knowledge among men.

[As finally adopted and made a law.].

James Smithson, esquire, of London, in the Kingdom of Great Britain,
having by his last will and testament given the whole of his property to the
United States of America, to found at Washington, under the name of the
"Smithsonian Institution," an establishment for the increase and diffusion
of knowledge among men; and the United States having, by an act of Con-
gress, received said property and accepted said trust; Therefore, for the
faithful execution of said trust, according to the will of the liberal and en-
lightened donor --
    Be it enacted by the Senate and House of Representatives of the United
States of America in Congress assembled, That the President and Vice-
President of the United States, the Secretary of State, the Secretary of the
Treasury, the Secretary of War, the Secretary of the Navy, the Postmaster-
General, the Attorney-General, the Chief Justice, and the Commissioner of
the Patent Office of the United States, and the mayor of the city of Washington, during the time for which they shall hold their respective offices, and
such other persons as they may elect honorary members, be, and they are
hereby constituted, an "establishment," by the name of the "Smithsonian
Institution," for the increase and diffusion of knowledge among men; and by
that name shall be known and have perpetual succession, with the powers,
limitations, and restrictions, hereinafter contained, and no other.
    Sec. 2. And be it further enacted, That so much of the property of the
said James Smithson as has been received in money, and paid into the treasury of the United States, being the sum of five hundred and fifteen thousand
one hundred and sixty-nine dollars, be lent to the United States treasury at

six per cent per annum interest, from the first day of September, in the
year one thousand eight hundred and thirty-eight, when the same was received into the said treasury; and that so much of the interest as may have
accrued on said sum on the first day of July next, which will amount to the
sum of two hundred and forty-two thousand one hundred and twenty-nine dollars, or so much thereof as shall by the Board of Regents of the Institution
established by this act be deemed necessary, be, and the same is hereby,
appropriated for the erection of suitable buildings, and for other current
incidental expenses of said Institution; and that six per cent. interest on the
said trust fund, it being the said amount of five hundred and fifteen thousand
one hundred and sixty-nine dollars, received into the United States treasury on the first of September, one thousand eight hundred and thirty-eight,
payable, in half-yearly payments, on the first of January and July in each
year, be, and the same is hereby, appropriated for the perpetual maintenance and support of said Institution; and all expenditures and appropriations to be made from time to time, to the purposes of the Institution aforesaid, shall be exclusively from the accruing interest, and not from the principal of the said fund. And be it further enacted, That all the moneys and
stocks which have been, or may hereafter be, received into the treasury
of the United States on account of the fund bequeathed by James Smithson,
be, and the same hereby are, pledged to refund to the treasury of the United
States the sums hereby appropriated.

Sec. 3. And be it further enacted, That the business of the said Institution shall be conducted at the city of Washington by a board of regents, by
the name of the Regents of the "Smithsonian Institution," to be composed of
the Vice-President of the United States, the Chief Justice of the United
States, and the mayor of the city of Washington, during the time for which
they shall hold their repsective offices; three members of the Senate, and
three members of the House of Representatives; together with six other
persons, other than members of Congress, two of whom shall be members
of the National Institute in the city of Washington, and resident in the said
city; and the other four thereof shall be inhabitants of States, and no two of
them of the same State. . . . .

Sec. 4. And be it further enacted, That, after the board of regents
shall have met and become organized, it shall be their duty forthwith to proceed to select a suitable site for such building as may be necessary for the
institution, which ground may be taken and appropriated out of that part of
the public ground in the city of Washington lying between the patent office
and Seventh Street: Provided, The President of the United States, the Secretary of State, the Secretary of the Treasury, the Secretary of War, the Secretary of the Navy, and the Commissioner of the Patent Office, shall consent to the same; but, if the persons last named shall not consent, then such
location may be made upon any other of the public grounds within the city of
Washington, belonging to the United States, which said regents may select,
. . . .

WASHINGTON LOSES ALEXANDRIA
1846

The District of Columbia's territorial limits were
reduced by one-third when Congress, upon a request of the state of Virginia, retroceded the county
of Alexandria to Virginia. The selection that follows is the Act of Retrocession.

Source: District of Columbia Code, 1967 Ed., Vol. I.

ACT OF RETROCESSION OF COUNTY OF ALEXANDRIA

AN ACT To retrocede the county of Alexandria, in the District of Columbia,
     to the State of Virginia

     Whereas no more territory ought to be held under the exclusive legis-
lation given to Congress over the District which is the seat of the General
Government than may be necessary and proper for the purposes of such a
seat; and whereas experience hath shown that the portion of the District of
Columbia ceded to the United States by the State of Virginia has not been,
nor is ever likely to be, necessary for that purpose; and whereas the State
of Virginia, by an act passed on the third day of February, eighteen hundred
and forty-six, entitled "An act accepting by the State of Virginia the county
of Alexandria, in the District of Columbia, when the same shall be receded
by the Congress of the United States," has signified her willingness to take
back the said territory ceded as aforesaid: Therefore,
     Be it enacted by the Senate and House of Representatives of the United
States of America in Congress assembled, That with the assent of the people
of the county and town of Alexandria, to be ascertained as hereinafter prescribed, all of that portion of the District of Columbia, ceded to the United
States by the State of Virginia, and all the rights and jurisdiction therewith
ceded over the same, be, and the same are hereby, ceded and forever re-
linquished to the State of Virginia, in full and absolute right and jurisdiction,
as well of soil as of persons residing or to reside thereon.
     SEC. 2. And be it further enacted, That nothing herein contained shall
be construed to vest in the State of Virginia any right of property in the cus-
tom-house and post-office of the United States within the town of Alexandria,
or in the soil of the territory hereby re-ceded, so as to affect the rights of
individuals or corporations therein, otherwise than as the same shall or
may be transferred by such individuals or corporations to the State of Virginia . . . .

THE FOURTH CHARTER
1848

> Congress granted the city its fourth charter. The
> most important provisions of this new act concerned
> the abolition of the property qualification for voting.
> White manhood suffrage was finally granted to the
> residents of the District in local elections.

Source: District of Columbia Code, 1967 Edition, Vol. I, Washington, D.C.,
1967 .

AN ACT To continue, alter and amend the charter of the city of Washington.

Be it enacted by the Senate and House of Representatives of the United
States of America in Congress assembled, That the act of May fifteenth,
eighteen hundred and twenty, entitled "An Act to incorporate the inhabitants
of the city of Washington, and to repeal all acts of May twenty-sixth, eighteen hundred and twenty-four, entitled "An Act supplementary to 'An Act to
incorporate the inhabitants of the city of Washington,' passed the fifteenth
of May, one thousand eight hundred and twenty, and for other purposes, "
and the act or acts supplemental or additional to said acts which were in
force on the fourteenth day of May, eighteen hundred and forty, or which
may, at the passing of this act, be in force, be and the same are hereby
continued in force for the term of twenty years from the date hereof, or
until Congress shall by law determine otherwise, with the alterations, ad-
ditions, explanations, and amendments following, that is to say:

SEC. 2. And be it further enacted, That the said corporation shall
have full power and authority to lay and collect a tax of not exceeding three
fourths of one per centum per annum upon the assessed value of all stocks
which may be owned and possessed by any person whatever in any banking
insurance, or other incorporated or unincorporated company in the city of
Washington; and to compel all such banking, insurance, or other incorporated or unincorporated company to furnish, when so required to do, within
ten days thereafter, a full and complete list of the names of the stockholders
in such company, and the amount of stock owned by each under a penalty not
exceeding fifty dollars for each and every week such company shall neglect
or refuse or fail to furnish the same. And in default of payment of the tax
due on said stock by the banking, insurance or other company, or by the
holder or holders of the stock, the said corporation shall have full power
and authority to sell the said stock, or so many shares thereof, and costs
of collection, as provided in the case of personal property. The said corporation shall also have power to lay and collect a tax not exceeding three

fourths of one per centum per annum on the assessed value of all bonds and
mortgages, of stocks of all kinds, and all public and private securities, and
on every description of property within the said city, or which may be owned
or held by the inhabitants thereof, except the wearing apparel and necessary
tools and implements used in carrying on the trade or occupation of any person; and to compel persons to furnish, when required by the assessors, a
full and correct list of all property by law taxable, held by them, and to
punish with suitable fines and penalties persons refusing or omitting to furnish such lists. The said corporation shall have power to lay and collect
a school-tax upon every free white male citizen of the age of twenty-one
years and upwards, of one dollar per annum; to provide for licensing, tax-
ing and regulating livery stables, and wholesale and retail dealers, in a ratio according to the annual average amount of the capital invested in the
business of such wholesale and retail dealers; to license, tax and regulate
agencies of all kinds of insurance companies; to tax private bankers, brokers and money lenders, not exceeding three fourths of one per centum per
annum on the assessed amount of capital employed in the business of said
private bankers, brokers and money lenders; to make all necessary regulations respecting hackney carriages and the rates of fare of the same, and
the rates of hauling by cartmen, wagoners, carmen, and draymen, and the
rates of commission of auctioneers; to regulate and graduate the licenses
of nonresident merchants and traders, and the taxes on the same; to regulate and establish fish wharves and docks; to restrain and prohibit gaming-
houses, and bawdy-houses; to punish those who may sell intoxicating liquors
without having obtained license therefor, by fines not less than five dollars;
and in default of the payment thereof, by imprisonment and labor in the
workhouse for a term not exceeding ninety days; to provide for the punish-
ing by fines and penalties, and by confinement to labor in the workhouse,
any person and all persons who shall molest or disturb any church or other
place of worship while the congregation are engaged in any religious exercise or proceedings; to provide for the weighing of all kinds of live stock
brought into the city; to cause to be pulled down unsafe, dilapidated, or
dangerous buildings; to take up and relay foot pavements and paved carriage-
ways, and to keep them in repair, and to lay and collect taxes for paying
the expenses thereof, on the property fronting on such foot-ways and carri-
age-ways; to lay and collect taxes for the support of public schools; to
cause new alleys to be opened into the squares, and to open, change, or
close those already laid out, upon the application of the owners of more
than one half of the property in such squares, subject to the second proviso
of the eighth section of the act of May the fifteenth, eighteen hundred and
twenty, incorporating the inhabitants of the city of Washington. And the
said corporation shall have full power and authority to make all necessary
laws for the protection of public and private property, the preservation of
order, the safety of persons, and, the observance of decency in the streets,
avenues, alleys, public spaces, and other places in the said city, and for
the punishment of all persons violating the same, as well as for the punishment of persons guilty of public profanity and prostitution.

SEC. 3. <u>And be it further enacted</u>, That at the first general election held after the passage of this act, a Board of Assessors, to consist of one member from each ward, shall be elected by the qualified voters therein, to serve for two years; and the returns of election for assessors shall be made in the same manner and form as the returns of the election for members of the Board of Aldermen and Board of Common Council; and the person having the greatest number of legal votes in each ward for assessor, shall be duly elected assessor; but in case two or more persons, highest in vote, shall have an equal number of votes, the commissioners of election for the ward in which such equality shall exist, shall decide the choice by lot. No person who is not eligible to a seat in the Board of Aldermen or Board of Common Council, shall be eligible to election as assessor. And on the first Monday of May next succeeding the first election of assessors under this act, the said board, or a majority of the members thereof, shall meet in the City Hall, and in the presence of the mayor and register, shall draw by lot the names of three members thereof, if the number of wards be seven, or if the number of wards exceed seven, the names of one half, as near as may be, of the members of said board; and the members whose names shall be thus drawn, shall thereupon cease to be members of said board; and at the next general election a member shall be elected to serve for two years in each of the wards in which the members so drawn shall have been elected; and at every regular annual election thereafter in such wards as the time of the assessors is about to expire, an assessor shall be elected to serve for two years. No person holding any other office under the corporation, shall be elected to or hold the office of assessor. In the event of the death, resignation, inability, or refusal to serve of any person elected an assessor, the vacancy shall be filled immediately by the Board of Aldermen and Board of Common Council, in joint meeting, in which manner all vacancies in the board of assessors shall be filled: <u>Provided</u>, That until the assessors authorized to be elected by this act, shall have been duly elected and qualified to enter upon their duties, full power and authority are hereby given to the said corporation to provide for the temporary appointment of assessors to perform the duties required of the assessors to be elected under this act. The board of assessors shall assess and value, and make return of all and every species of property by law taxable, at such times, and under such regulations, as the said corporation shall prescribe; and if the said assessors, or either of them, or come to their knowledge, or shall refuse or wilfully neglect to make return of any person subject to a school-tax, they, or the one so offending, shall be subject to a fine not exceeding one hundred dollars for each offence, at the discretion of the Circuit Court of the District of Columbia for the county of Washington, and shall thereafter be incapable of holding any office under the corporation; and the Board of Aldermen and Board of Common Council may, by joint resolution, remove any assessor from office for any misconduct in office.

SEC. 4. <u>And be it further enacted</u>, That the register, collector, and

surveyor of the said city shall severally be elected on the first Monday in
June next, and on the same day in every second year thereafter, at the same
time and place, and in the same manner, and by the persons qualified to
vote for mayor and members of the Board of Aldermen and Board of Common Council: Provided, That if the said first Monday in June next shall be
the regular day for the election of mayor of the said city, then the next
election thereafter, of register, collector, and surveyor, shall take place
on the same day in the following year, and then on the same day in every
second year thereafter, as above provided; and the commissioners of election shall make out duplicate certificates of the result of the election for
register, collector, and surveyor, and shall return one to the Board of Aldermen, and the other to the Board of Common Council on the Monday next
ensuing the day of election; and the persons having the greatest number of
votes for those offices respectively, shall be register, collector, or surveyor, as the case may be; but in case two or more persons highest in vote
shall have an equal number of votes for either of said offices, then it shall
be lawful for the Board of Aldermen and Board of Common Council to proceed forthwith by ballot, in joint meeting, to determine the choice between
such persons; and the said register, collector and surveyor shall respectively hold their offices until their respective successors are duly elected
and qualified, unless sooner removed from office; and full power and authority are hereby granted to the Corporation of Washington to pass all such
laws as may be necessary to define and regulate the respective duties, powers, and authority of the said register, collector, and surveyor; and also
to prescribe the amount of bond and security to be given to the said corporation by each before entering upon the duties of their respective offices, and
generally to pass all such laws as may be necessary to insure an efficient
and faithful discharge of the duties of their respective offices, by the said
register, collector, and surveyor; and in case the said officers, or either
of them, shall fail or refuse to comply with any law, resolution, or order
of the said corporation, or shall fail or refuse to obey any order of the
mayor of the said city, or shall fail to discharge the duties of their respective offices with fidelity and a strict regard to the interests of the said corporation, or shall prove unable or incompetent, from any cause whatever,
to discharge such duties, or shall be guilty of any malversation in office,
or shall be convicted of any high crime or misdemeanor, it shall be lawful
for the majority of the Board of Aldermen and Board of Common Council,
by joint resolution, to remove such officer, and to order an election to fill
the vacancy; and in case of the refusal or failure of any person elected to
either of said offices to accept of the same, or to give such bond and security as may be required by said corporation within twenty days after his election, or in case of the death, resignation, or removal from the said city of
any person elected to or holding either of said offices, it shall be lawful for
the Board of Aldermen and Board of Common Council to declare said office
vacant, and to order an election to fill the vacancy. And in all cases where
it shall become necessary to hold an election to fill a vacancy in either of

said offices, the same regulations shall be observed as to the appointment of commissioners to hold said elections, and as to holding the elections and the returns of the same, as are observed at the regular elections; <u>Provided,</u> That authority is hereby given to the mayor of the said city to appoint temporarily, under such regulations as the said corporation may prescribe, some discreet person to discharge the duties of such vacant office until an election can be had and a successor duly elected and qualified to enter upon his duties.

SEC. 5. <u>And be it further enacted,</u> That every free white male citizen of the United States, who shall have attained the age of twenty-one years and shall have resided in the city of Washington one year immediately preceding the day of election, and shall be a resident of the ward in which he shall offer to vote, and shall have been returned on the books of the corporation during the year ending the thirty-first of December next preceding the day of election as subject to a school-tax for that year, (except persons <u>non compos mentis</u>, vagrants, paupers, or persons who shall have been convicted of any infamous crime,) and who shall have paid the school-taxes, and all taxes on personal property due from him, shall be entitled to vote for mayor, members of the Board of Aldermen and Board of Common Council, and assessors, and for every officer authorized to be elected at any election under this act, or the act or acts to which this is amendatory or supplementary: <u>Provided,</u> That if, during the year ending on the thirty-first day of December next preceding the day of the first election after the passage of this act, no persons shall have been returned on the books of the said corporation as subject to a school-tax before the day of the said first election, and who shall in all other respects be qualified under this act to vote, and who shall have paid the said school-tax and all taxes due on personal property, shall be entitled to vote at the said first election after the passage of this act. And if any person shall buy or sell a vote, or shall vote more than once at any corporation election, held in pursuance of law, or shall give or receive any consideration therefor in money, goods, or any other thing of value, or shall promise any valuable consideration, or vote in consideration of such promise, he shall be disqualified forever thereafter from voting and holding any office under said corporation; and on complaint thereof to the attorney of the United States for the District of Columbia, it shall be the duty of said attorney to proceed against such offender or offenders by indictment and trial, as in other criminal cases; and if found guilty, it shall be the duty of the court to sentence him to pay a fine of not less than ten dollars, and to imprisonment not more than two months nor less than ten days . . . .

THE SLAVE TRADE IS ABOLISHED -- 1850

As part of the Compromise of 1850, the Slave Trade, but not
slavery, in the District of Columbia was abolished. At the time,
this Congressional Act was considered a great victory for abo-
litionism, although many Washingtonians accepted the measure
grudgingly.

Source: United States Statutes at Large, vol. 9, pp. 467-468.

AN ACT to Suppress the Slave Trade in the District of Columbia.

Be it Enacted by the Senate and House of Representatives of the
United States of America in Congress assembled, That from and after
the first day of January, eighteen hundred and fifty-one, it shall not
be lawful to bring into the District of Columbia any slave whatever,
for the purpose of being sold, or for the purpose of being placed in
depot to be subsequently transferred to any other State or place to be sold
as merchandize. And if any slave shall be brought into the said District
by its owner, or by the authority or consent of its owner, contrary to
the provisions of this act, such slave shall thereupon become liberated
and free.

Sec. 2. And be it further enacted, That it shall and may be lawful
for each of the corporations of the cities of Washington and Georgetown, from time to time, and as often as may be necessary, to abate,
break up, and abolish any depot or place of confinement of slaves
brought into the said District as merchandize, contrary to the provisions of this act, by such appropriate means as may appear to either
of the said corporations expedient and proper. And the same power
is hereby vested in the Levy Court of Washington county, if any attempt
shall be made, within its jurisdictional limits, to establish a depot
or place of confinement for slaves brought into the said District as
merchandize for sale contrary to this act.

APPROVED, September 20, 1850.

A POLICE DEPARTMENT FOR WASHINGTON
1851

Despite the city's continued growth, it did not
receive a uniformed and salaried police department until March, 1851, when the city council
passed an act establishing a new law enforcement system for the city.

Source: Laws of the Corporation of the City of Washington, 48th Council,
Washington, 1851.

Be it enacted by the Board of Aldermen and Board of Common Council
of the city of Washington, That the City of Washington be and the same is
hereby divided into seven police districts, as follows: The First Ward to
constitute the First District; the Second Ward the Second District; the Third
Ward the Third District; the Fourth Ward the Fourth District; the Fifth
Ward the Fifth District; the Sixth Ward the Sixth District; and the Seventh
Ward the Seventh District.

SEC. 2. And be it enacted, That immediately after the passage of this
act, and annually thereafter, on or about the fourth Monday in June, the
Mayor shall appoint, by and with the advice and consent of the Board of Aldermen, two police officers for each of the First, Second, Third, Fifth, Sixth,
and Seventh Police Districts, and three for the Fourth District, who shall,
each in their respective districts, promptly and strictly enforce the police
regulations and penal ordinances of this Corporation, and the laws of the
United States, as they now are or may hereafter exist: Provided, That it
shall be the duty of a police officer of one district to render his assistance
in another district, (under regulations hereafter provided for,) whenever
necessary, or whenever directed by the Mayor: And provided further, That
no police officer appointed under this act shall be engaged in any other business or calling except the duties of his office as prescribed by this act:
And provided further, That said officers shall remain on duty to such hour
in the night as may be fixed for the commencement of the night watch.

SEC. 3. And be it enacted, That in lieu of all fees, fines, forfeitures,
&c., of every kind or nature whatsoever, (except such legal fees as shall,
in pursuance of law, accrue to them in the execution of the laws of the United
States,) the compensation of each of the police officers shall be five hundred
dollars per annum, payable monthly out of the general fund, (under restrictions and provisions to be hereafter provided for; and before any police officer shall enter upon the duties of his office, he shall give bond, with two
good and sufficient sureties, to this Corporation, to be approved by the Mayor, in the sum of one thousand dollars, for the faithful execution of his duties, and the prompt payment to this Corporation of all moneys which may

come into his hands as fees, fines,forfeitures, &c., at such times as may be prescribed by law; and no police officer appointed under this act shall exact any fee, or receive any fee, reward, or emolument, or compensation whatever, for the execution of any duty which he may be legally required to perform, except such reward as may from time to time be publicly offered by the authorities of any other municipal Corporation or State, or by the authorities of the United States: Provided, That in case the Mayor shall order an officer to leave the city in discharge of his duty, then his actual expenses shall be paid by this Corporation.

SEC. 4. And be it enacted, That immediately after the passage of this act, and annually thereafter, on or about the fourth Monday in June, the Board of Aldermen and Board of Common Council shall meet in joint meeting and select from the magistrates of the county of Washington, one police magistrate for each of the several police districts of this city; who, before entering upon his duties, shall be a resident of the District, and keep his office therein, at such convenient point as the Mayor shall approve; and who shall, each in his respective district, perform all the duties which now are or may hereafter be required of the several police magistrates by the laws of this Corporation: Provided, That it shall be the duty of a police magistrate of one district to render his assistance in the preservation of the peace or the execution of the laws of this Corporation in any other district, (under regulations hereafter provided for, whenever necessary, or whenever directed by the Mayor: And provided further, That no member of either Board of the City Council shall be selected as a police magistrate under this act.

SEC. 5. And be it enacted, That in lieu of all fees, fines, costs, &c., which may now or hereafter accrue to the police magistrates under the laws of this Corporation, the several police magistrates selected under this act shall receive annually the following compensation, payable monthly out of the general fund, viz: the police magistrates of the First, Second, Third, Fifth, Sixth, and Seventh Police Districts, three hundred and fifty dollars each; and the police magistrate of the Fourth District, five hundred dollars, (under restrictions and provisions to be hereafter provided for;) and before any police magistrate shall enter upon the duties of his office, he shall give bond with two good and sufficient sureties to this Corporation, to be approved by the Mayor, in the sum of one thousand dollars, for the faithful execution of his duties and the prompt payment to this Corporation of all moneys which may come into his hands as fees, fines, costs, &c., at such times as may be prescribed by law.

SEC. 6. And be it enacted, That the Mayor, by and with the advice and consent of the Board of Aldermen, shall appoint, at the time named in the second section of this act, and annually thereafter, some suitable person, to be, and who is hereby constituted, under the control and direction of the Mayor, the Chief of the Police of the city of Washington . . . .

THE METROPOLITAN POLICE DISTRICT
1861

As a result of the outbreak of the Civil War, Congress believed that the nation's capital needed greater security. Therefore, in August 1861, it created a new metropolitan police force and board under federal control.

Source: U.S. Laws and Statutes, Compilation of the Laws in Force in the District of Columbia, Washington, 1868.

Be it enacted by the Senate and House of Representatives of the United States of America in Congress assembled, That the corporations of Washington and Georgetown, and the county of Washington, outside of the limits of said corporations, are hereby constituted, for the purposes of this act, into one district, to be called "The Metropolitan Police district of the District of Columbia."

SEC. 2. And be it further enacted, That immediately upon the passage of this act, and thereafter from time to time, as required by this act, there shall be appointed by the President of the United States, by and with the advice and consent of the Senate, five commissioners of police, who shall be the chief officers of the said "Metropolitan Police district," and who shall severally possess and perform therein the powers and duties authorized and enjoined by this act. The said commissioners, together with the mayors of the cities of Washington and Georgetown, ex officio, shall form the Board of Police for the said district, and a majority of them shall constitute a quorum of such board for the transaction of business.

SEC. 3. And be it further enacted, That three of said commissioners shall be appointed from the city of Washington, one from Georgetown, and one from the county of Washington at large, for the term of three years, and until their successors are appointed and qualified, unless sooner removed by the President. The said commissioners shall meet at such time and place as may be designated by the President of the United States; and after being duly qualified, by taking and subscribing an oath or affirmation before some person duly authorized to administer oaths in said District, to support the Constitution of the United States, and faithfully to discharge the duties of his office, shall proceed to discharge such duties as [are] prescribed by this act.

SEC. 4. And be it further enacted, That the officers of the Board of Police shall be a president and a treasurer, who shall each be selected from among said commissioners by themselves, who shall discharge such duties as the board may prescribe. The treasurer shall give a bond, with two sureties, to the satisfaction of said board, in the penal sum of ten thousand dollars, for the faithful discharge of the duties of his office. The board may also appoint a clerk, to hold his office during the pleasure of the board, and to receive a compensation to be fixed by the board, not to exceed the rate of one thousand dollars per annum, and who shall perform such duties as may be required by said Board of Police.

SEC. 5. And be it further enacted, That it shall be the duty of the Board of Police hereby constituted, at all times of the day and night, within the boundaries of the said police district, to preserve the public peace; to prevent crime, and arrest offenders; to protect the rights of persons and of property; to guard the public health; to preserve order at every public election; to remove nuisances existing in the public streets, roads, alleys, highways, and other places; to provide a proper police force at every fire, in order that thereby the firemen and property may be protected; to protect strangers and travellers at steamboat and ship landings and railway stations; to see that all laws relating to the observance of Sunday, and regarding pawnbrokers, mock auctions, elections, gambling, intemperance, lottery dealers, vagrants, disorderly persons, and the public health, are promptly enforced, and to enforce and obey all laws and ordinances of the city councils of the cities of Washington and Georgetown which are properly applicable to police or health, and not inconsistent with the provisions of this act.

SEC. 6. And be it further enacted, That the duties of the Board of Police shall be more especially executed under the direction and control of said board, and according to rules and regulations which it is hereby authorized to pass, from time to time, for the proper government and discipline of its subordinate officers, by a police force for the whole of said police district, and authorized to do duty in any part thereof, without regard to residence or corporation lines.

SEC. 7. And be it further enacted, That the said police force shall consist of a superintendent of police, ten sergeants of police, and such number of police patrolmen as the board may deem necessary, not exceeding, for the regular service, one hundred and fifty. The said offices hereby created for the said police force shall be severally filled by appointment from the board of police; and each person so appointed shall hold office only during such time as he shall faithfully observe and execute all the rules and regulations of the said board, the laws of the United States, and the laws or ordinances existing within the District, enacted by the city or county authorities within the same, and which laws or ordinances apply to such part of the District where the members of the police force may be on duty.

SEC. 8. And be it further enacted, That the qualifications, enumeration, and distribution of duties, mode of trial, and removal from office of each officer of said police force shall be particularly defined and prescribed by rules and regulations of the Board of Police, in accordance with the Constitution and laws of the United Sates applicable thereto: Provided, however, That no person shall be so appointed to office, or hold office in the police force aforesaid, who cannot read and write the English language. . . .

EMANCIPATION IN THE DISTRICT OF COLUMBIA
1862

The question of slavery in the nation's capital
was one of long concern and never ending de-
bate. In 1862 Congress passed an act freeing
the slaves of the District. The following selection is the statement made by President Abraham Lincoln upon his signing of this measure.

Source: James D. Richardson, comp. and ed., Messages and Papers of the
Presidents, VII, New York, 1897.

April 16, 1862.

Fellow-Citizens of the Senate and House of Representatives:

The act entitled "An act for the release of certain persons held to service or labor in the District of Columbia" has this day been approved and
signed.

I have never doubted the constitutional authority of Congress to abolish
slavery in this District, and I have ever desired to see the national capital
freed from the institution in some satisfactory way. Hence there has never
been in my mind any question upon the subject except the one of expediency,
arising in view of all the circumstances. If there be matters within and
about this act which might have taken a course or shape more satisfactory
to my judgment, I do not attempt to specify them. I am gratified that the
two principles of compensation and colonization are both recognized and
practically applied in the act.

In the matter of compensation, it is provided that claims may be presented within ninety days from the passage of the act, "but not thereafter;"
and there is no saving for minors, femes covert, insane or absent persons.
I presume this is an omission by mere oversight, and I recommend that it
be supplied by an amendatory or supplemental act.

ABRAHAM LINCOLN.

HIGHWAYS FOR THE CAPITAL
1862

>While other urban services may have been ne-
>glected in Washington, the building, repair, and
>maintenance of streets, roads, and highways in
>the city seems to have been of major concern.
>By 1875, as a matter of record, Washington was
>one of the best paved cities in the world. The
>following selection is typical of the many acts
>passed by Congress relating to street and high-
>way construction.

Source: District of Columbia Code, 1967 Ed., vol. I.

AN ACT Relating to highways in the county of Washington and District of Columbia

Be it enacted by the Senate and House of Representatives of the United States of America in Congress assembled, That from and after the passage of this act, it shall be lawful for the levy court of Washington county, in the District of Columbia, to alter, repair, widen, and regulate the public roads and highways in said county, and to lay out additional roads as hereinafter specified.

SEC. 2. And be it further enacted, That all roads within said county of Washington which have been used by the public for a period of twenty-five years or more as a highway, and have been recognized by the said levy court as public county roads, and for the repairs of which the said levy court has appropriated and expended money, are declared public highways, whether the same have been recorded or not; and any person who shall obstruct the free use of said highways, or any one of them, without authority from said levy court, shall be subject to a fine for each and every offence of not less than one hundred or more than two hundred and fifty dollars, to be imprisoned till the said fine and the costs of suit and collection of the same are paid; said fines to be collected in the name of the United States, for the use of the levy court.

SEC. 3. And be it further enacted, That within one year from the passage of this act the levy court shall cause the surveyor of the said county of Washington to survey and plat all such roads as are named in the last preceding section, and have the same recorded among the records. . . .

SEC. 7. And be it further enacted, That said corporation shall have power and authority to repair any of the footways of the streets in said town, and to impose and collect such tax or taxes on the lot or lots, or parts thereof, adjoining the same, as may be necessary to pay the expense of such repairs. . . .

A FIRE DEPARTMENT FOR WASHINGTON
1864

In the expanding cities of the nineteenth century,
the threat of fire was always an important urban
problem. Washington, like other American cities,
had depended upon voluntary fire companies to con-
tend with this urban service. In February 1864,
however, the city council finally abolished the
volunteer companies and established a paid and
uniformed fire department. The act creating
this new municipal organization follows.

Source: William B. Webb, ed., The Laws of the Corporation of the City
of Washington . . . Containing a Digest of the Charter and Other Acts of
Congress Concerning the City, Washington, D.C., 1868.

FIRE DEPARTMENT.

1. The Mayor shall appoint, as other city officers are appointed, four
persons of good character and standing, who shall be, in conjunction with
the Mayor, styled the "Fire Commissioners of the City of Washington."

2. Should any one or more of said Commissioners refuse or neglect to
perform the duties of the office to which they have been appointed, the Mayor being duly certified thereof by any two of said Commissioners, shall
fill such office by new appointment, to serve for the full term of those refusing or neglecting to serve; and should any vacancy occur the Mayor shall
fill the same by new appointment.

3. There shall be appointed, as other city officers are appointed, a
clerk, who, by virtue of his office, shall be a member of the Fire Department, and shall receive a salary of seven hundred dollars per annum, but
shall not be entitled to any other pay under the law creating the Fire Department, and who shall perform the duties of a clerk to the Chief Engineer.

4. The Fire Commissioners shall have power to appoint the persons re-
quisite to perform the duties prescribed by the law organizing the Fire Department except the Chief Engineer, which persons shall hold their positions
during good behavior; to suspend or expel any member of any company, and
to adopt a suitable uniform to be worn by the officers and men of the Department.

The Fire Commissioners shall adopt such rules and regulations for their
own government and for the government of the Fire Department as they
shall deem expedient for the interests of said department, provided they
are not inconsistent with the laws of the Corporation; they shall keep a record of all their proceedings subject to the inspection of the Mayor and City

Councils, and they shall prescribe the duties of their clerk.

5. The Fire Department shall consist of a Chief Engineer, three steam fire engine companies, each to consist of one foreman, one engineer, one fireman, one hostler, and six extra-men; one hook and ladder company, to consist of one foreman, one hostler, one tillerman, and six extra-men, and as many supernumeraries to each company as the Commissioners may deem necessary.

6. The steam engine companies shall have one steam enginee, one hose-reel or cart, three horses, and one thousand feet of hose.

7. The hook and ladder company shall be provided with one truck, two horses, and as many hooks and ladders, &c., as the Commissioners may determine.

8. The salaries of the officers and men comprising this Deparmtnet shall be as follows, per annum, payable monthly out of the General Fund, viz: The Chief Engineer shall receive fifteen hundred dollars; the engineer of each company, nine hundred dollars; the foreman, three hundred and fifty dollars; the tillerman, seven hundred dollars; the fireman and hostler, seven hundred dollars each; and the extra-men two hundred dollars each; the said extra-men shall uniform themselves. . . .

A WASHINGTON CIVIL RIGHTS ACT
1869

On June 10, 1869, the Washington city council
passed the first Civil Rights Act in the city's
history. Although not all Washingtonians approved of the measure, most of the residents
grudgingly agreed to abide by its provisions.

Source: Laws of the Corporation of the City of Washington passed by the
Sixty-Sixth Council, vol. 13, Washington, D.C., 1869.

AN ACT regulating admission to places of public amusement and entertainment.

   Be it enacted by the Board of Aldermen and Board of Common Council of
the City of Washington, That from and after the passage of this act it shall
not be lawful for any person or persons who shall have obtained a license
from this Corporation for the purpose of giving a lecture, concert, exhibition, circus performance, theatrical entertainment, or for conducting a
place of public amusement of any kind, to make any distinction on account
of race or color, as regards the admission of persons to any part of the
hall or audience-room where such lecture, concert, exhibition, or other
entertainment may be given: Provided, That any person applying shall pay
the regular price charged for admission to such part of the house as he or
she may wish to occupy, and shall conduct himself or herself in an orderly
and peaceable manner, while on the premises; and any person or persons
offending herein shall forfeit and pay to this Corporation for each offence
a fine of not less than ten nor more than twenty dollars, to be collected and
applied as are other fines.
   SEC. 2. And be it further enacted, That all acts or parts of acts inconsistent with this act be, and the same are hereby,repealed.
   Approved June 10, 1869.

THE DISTRICT TERRITORIAL ACT
1871

Congress passed the District Territorial Act
ending municipal government in Washington
and the District of Columbia. Henceforth, the
city and the District would be governed by a
presidentially appointed governor and council.

Source: District of Columbia Code, 1967 Edition, vol. I, Washington, D.C.,
1967.

Be it enacted by the Senate and House of Representatives of the United
States of America in Congress assembled, That all part of the territory
of the United States included within the limits of the District of Columbia
be, and the same is hereby, created into a government by the name of the
District of Columbia, by which name it is hereby constituted a body corporate for municipal purposes, and may contract and be contracted with, sue
and be sued, plead and be impleaded, have a seal, and exercise all other
powers of a municipal corporation not inconsistent with the Constitution and
laws of the United States and the provisions of this act.

SEC. 2. And be it further enacted, That the executive power and authority in and over said District of Columbia shall be vested in a governor,who
shall be appointed by the President, by and with the advice and consent of
the Senate, and who shall hold his office for four years, and until his successor shall be appointed and qualified. The governor shall be a citizen of
and shall have resided within said District twelve months before his appointment, and have the qualifications of an elector. He may grant pardons and
respites for offenses against the laws of said District enacted by the legislative assembly thereof; he shall commission all officers who shall be elected
or appointed to office under the laws of the said District enacted as aforesaid, and shall take care that the laws be faithfully executed.

SEC. 3. And be it further enacted, That every bill which shall have
passed the council and house of delegates shall, before it becomes a law,
be presented to the governor of the District of Columbia; if he approve, he
shall sign it, but if not, he shall return it, with his objections, to the house
in which it shall have originated, who shall enter the objections at large on
their journal, and proceed to reconsider it. If, after such reconsideration,
two thirds of all the members appointed or elected to the house shall agree
to pass the bill, it shall be sent, together with the objections, to the other
house, by which it shall likewise be reconsidered, and if approved by two
thirds of all the members appointed or elected to that house, it shall become a law. But in all such cases the votes of both houses shall be determined by yeas and nays, and the names of the persons voting for and against

the bill shall be entered on the journal of each house respectively. If any
bill shall not be returned by the governor within ten days (Sundays excepted)
after it shall have been presented to him, the same shall be a law in like
manner as if he had signed it, unless the legislative assembly by their adjournment prevent its return, in which case it shall not be a law.

SEC. 4. And be it further enacted, That there shall be appointed by the
President, by and with the advice and consent of the Senate, a secretary of
said District, who shall reside therein and possess the qualification of an
elector, and shall hold his office for four years, and until his successor
shall be appointed and qualified; he shall record and preserve all laws and
proceedings of the legislative assembly hereinafter constituted, and all the
acts and proceedings of the governor in his executive department; he shall
transmit one copy of the laws and journals of the legislative assembly within thirty days after the end of each session, and one copy of the executive
proceedings and official correspondence semiannually, on the first days of
January and July in each year, to the President of the United States, and
four copies of the laws to the President of the Senate and to the Speaker of
the House of Representatives, for the use of Congress; and in case of the
death, removal, resignation, disability, or absence, of the governor from
the District, the secretary shall be, and he is hereby, authorized and required to execute and perform all the powers and duties of the governor during such vacancy, disability, or absence, or until another governor shall
be duly appointed and qualified to fill such vacancy. And in case the offices
of governor and secretary shall both become vacant, the powers, duties,
and emoluments of the office of governor shall devolve upon the presiding
officer of the council, and in case that office shall also be vacant, upon the
presiding officer of the house of delegates, until the office shall be filled
by a new appointment.

SEC. 5. And be it further enacted, That legislative power and authority
in said District shall be vested in a legislative assembly as hereinafter provided. The assembly shall consist of a council and house of delegates.
The council shall consist of eleven members, of whom two shall be residents of the city of Georgetown, and two residents of the county outside of
the cities of Washington and Georgetown, who shall be appointed by the
President, by and with the advice and consent of the Senate, who shall have
the qualification of voters as hereinafter prescribed, five of whom shall be
first appointed for the term of one year, and six for the period of two years,
provided that all subsequent appointments shall be for the term of two years.
The house of delegates shall consist of twenty-two members, possessing
the same qualifications as prescribed for the members of the council, whose
term of service shall continue one year. An apportionment shall be made
as nearly equal as practicable into eleven districts for the appointment of
the council, and into twenty-two districts for the election of delegates, giving to each section of the District representation in the ratio of its population as nearly as may be. And the members of the council and of the house
of delegates shall reside in and be inhabitants of the districts from which

they are appointed or elected, respectively. For the purposes of the first election to be held under this act, the governor and judges of the supreme court of the District of Columbia shall designate the districts for members of the house of delegates, appoint a board of registration and persons to superintend the election and returns thereof, prescribe the time, places, and manner of conducting such election, and make all needful rules and regulations for carrying into effect the provisions of the act not otherwise herein provided for: <u>Provided,</u> That the first election shall be held within sixty days from the passage of this act. In the first and all subsequent elections the persons having the highest number of legal votes for the house of delegates, respectively, shall be declared by the governor duly elected members of said house. In case two or more persons voted for shall have an equal number of votes for the same office, or if a vacancy shall occur in the house of delegates, the governor shall order a new election. And the persons thus appointed and elected to the legislative assembly shall meet at such time and at such place within the District as the governor shall appoint; but thereafter the time, place, and manner of holding and conducting all elections by the people, and the formation of the districts for members of the council and house of delegates, shall be prescribed by law, as well as the day of the commencement of the regular sessions of the legislative assembly: <u>Provided,</u>That no session in any one year shall exceed the term of sixty days, except the first session, which may continue one hundred days.

SEC. 6. <u>And</u> <u>be</u> <u>it</u> <u>further</u> <u>enacted,</u> That the legislative assembly shall have power to divide that portion of the District not included in the corporate limits of Washington or Georgetown into townships, not exceeding three, and create township officers, and prescribe the duties thereof; but all township officers shall be elected by the people of the townships respectively.
. . .

SEC. 19. <u>And</u> <u>be</u> <u>it</u> <u>further</u> <u>enacted,</u> That no member of the legislative assembly shall hold or be appointed to any office, which shall have been created or the salary or emoluments of which shall have been increased while he was a member, during the term for which he was appointed or elected, and for one year after the expiration of such term; and no person holding any office of trust or profit under the government of the United States shall be a member of the legislative assembly.

SEC. 20. <u>And</u> <u>be</u> <u>it</u> <u>further</u> <u>enacted,</u> That the said legislative assembly shall have no power to pass any ex post facto law, nor law impairing the obligation of contracts, nor to tax the property of the United States, nor to tax the lands or other property of non-residents higher than the lands or other property of residents; nor shall lands or other property in said district be liable to a higher tax, in any one year, for all general objects, territorial and municipal, than two dollars on every hundred dollars of the cash value thereof; but special taxes may be levied in particular sections, wards, or districts for their particular local improvements. . . .

INTEGRATED SCHOOLS IN WASHINGTON, D.C.
1871

> In 1871, the District of Columbia received a new
> charter. The section on education was very brief
> and made no mention of integrated schools for the
> capital. What follows is part of a speech made by
> a black senator from Mississippi, Hiram Revels,
> in which he pointed out that the black in Washing-
> ton, and throughout the country, wanted the oppor-
> tunity to live without special restrictions.

Source: Speech of Senator Hiram Revels, February 8, 1871, Congressional
Globe, 41st Congress, 3rd session, Part II, pp. 1059-1060.

In regard to the wishes of the colored people of this city I will simply
say that the trustees of colored schools and some of the most intelligent
colored men of this place have said to me that they would have before asked
for a bill abolishing the separate colored schools and putting all children
on an equality in the common schools if they had thought they could obtain
it. They feared they could not; and this is the only reason why they did not
ask for it before.

I find that the prejudice in this country to color is very great, and I
sometimes fear that it is on the increase. For example, let me remark
that it matters not how colored people act, it matters not how well they be-
have themselves, how well they deport themselves, how intelligent they
may be, how refined they may be -- for there are some colored persons
who are persons of refinement; this must be admitted -- the prejudice
against them is equally as great as it is against the most low and degraded
colored man you can find in the streets of this city or in any other place.

Mr. President, let me here remark that if this amendment is rejected,
so that the schools will be left open for all children to be entered into them,
irrespective of race, color, or previous condition, I do not believe the colored people will act imprudently. I know that in one or two of the late in-
surrectionary States the Legislatures passed laws establishing mixed
schools, and the colored people did not hurriedly shove their children into
those schools; they were very slow about it. In some localities where there
was but little prejudice or opposition to it they entered them immediately;
in others they did not do so. I do not believe that it is in the colored people
to act rashly and unwisely in a matter of this kind.

But, sir, let me say that it is the wish of the colored people of this District, and of the colored people over this land, that this Congress shall not
do anything which will increase that prejudice which is now fearfully great
against them. . . .

THE ORGANIC ACT FOR THE DISTRICT
1878

In 1878 Congress passed the Organic Act, by
which Washingtonians lost all self-government.
The administration of the city was placed in the
hands of three permanent commissioners appointed by the President. This form of government continued until 1961, when Washington
was once again given a municipal charter.

Source: District of Columbia Code, 1967 Edition, vol. I, Washington, D.C.,
1967.

Be it enacted by the Senate and House of Representatives of the United
States of America in Congress assembled, That all the territory which was
ceded by the State of Maryland to the Congress of the United States for the
permanent seat of the government of the United States shall continue to be
designated as the District of Columbia. Said District and the property and
persons that may be therein shall be subject to the following provisions
for the government of the same, and also to any existing laws applicable
thereto not hereby repealed or inconsistent with the provisions of this act.
The District of Columbia shall remain and continue a municipal corporation,
as provided in section two of the Revised Statutes relating to said District,
and the Commissioners herein provided for shall be deemed and taken as
officers of such corporation; and all laws now in force relating to the District of Columbia not inconsistent with the provisions of this act shall remain in full force and effect.

SEC. 2. That within twenty days after the approval of this act the President of the United States, by and with the advice and consent of the Senate,
is hereby authorized to appoint two persons, who, with an officer of the
Corps of Engineers of the United States Army, whose lineal rank shall be
above that of captain, shall be Commissioners of the District of Columbia,
and who, from and after July first, eighteen hundred and seventy-eight,
shall exercise all the powers and authority now vested in the Commissioners
of said District, except as are hereinafter limited or provided, and shall
be subject to all restrictions and limitations and duties which are not imposed upon said Commissioners. The Commissioner who shall be an officer detailed, from time to time, from the Corps of Engineers, by the President, for this duty, shall not be required to perform any other, nor shall
he receive any other compensation than his regular pay and allowances as
an officer of the Army. The two persons appointed from civil life shall, at
the time of their appointment, be citizens of the United States, and shall
have been actual residents of the District of Columbia for three years next

before their appointment, and have, during that period, claimed residence nowhere else, and one of said three Commissioners shall be chosen president of the Board of Commissi oners at their first meeting, and annually and whenever a vacancy shall occur, thereafter; and said Commissioners shall each of them, before entering upon the discharge of his duties, take an oath or affirmation to support the Constitution of the United States, and to faithfully discharge the duties imposed upon him by law; and said Commissioners appointed from civil life, shall each receive for his services a compensation at the rate of five thousand dollars per annum. The offical term of said Commissioners appointed from civil life shall be three years, and until their successors are appointed and qualified; but the first appointment shall be one Commissioner for one year and one for two years, and at the expiration of their respective terms their successors shall be appointed for three years. Neither of said Commissioners, nor any officer whatsoever of the District of Columbia, shall be accepted as surety upon any bond required to be given to the District of Columbia; nor shall any contractor be accepted as surety for any officer or other contractor in said District.

The said Commissioners are hereby authorized and empowered to determine which officers and employees of the District of Columbia, or which positions occupied or to be occupied by such officers and employees, shall hereafter be bonded for the faithful discharge of the duties of such officers and employees or of such positions, and to fix the penalty or penalties of any such bond: Provided, That this power of the Commissioners shall not apply to officers and employees who receive, disburse, account for, or otherwise are responsible for the handling of money, and whose bonds are now fixed by law. The provisions of the act of Congress entitled "An Act making appropriations to supply urgent deficiencies in appropriations for the fiscal year nineteen hundred and nine, and for other purposes, " approved August 5, 1909 (36 Stat. 118, 125 U.S.C., title 6, § 14), relating to rates of premiums for bonds for officers and employees of the United States shall be, and are hereby, made applicable to the rates of premiums for bonds of officers and employees of the government of the District of Columbia. (Amended June 28, 1935, 49 Stat. 430, ch. 332, § 1; July 7, 1955, 69 Stat, 281, ch. 280, § 1.)

SEC. 3. That as soon as the Commissioners appointed and detailed as aforesaid shall have taken and subscribed the oath or affirmation hereinbefore required, all the powers, rights, duties, and privileges lawfully exercised by, and all property, estate, and effects now vested by law in the Commissioners appointed under the provisions of the act of Congress approved June twentieth, eighteen hundred and seventy-four, shall be transferred to and vested in and imposed upon said Commissioners; and the functions of the Commissioners so appointed under the act of June twentieth, eighteen hundred and seventy-four, shall cease and determine. And the Commissioners of the District of Columbia shall have power, subject to the limitations and provisions herein contained, to apply the taxes or other revenues of said District to the payment of the current expenses thereof, to the support of the public schools, the fire department, and the police, and for that purpose shall take possession and supervision of all the offices, books, papers, records, moneys, credits, securities, assets, and accounts belonging or appertaining to the business or interests of the government of the District of Columbia, and exercise the duties, powers, and authority aforesaid; but said Commissioners, in the exercise of such duties, powers, and authority, shall make no contract, nor incur any obligation other than such contracts and obligations as are hereinafter provided for and shall be approved by Congress. The Commissioners shall have power to locate the places where hacks shall stand and change them as often as the public interests require. Any person violating any orders lawfully made in pursuance of this power shall be subject to a fine of not less than ten nor more than one hundred dollars, to be recovered before any justice of the peace in an action in the name of the Commissioners. All taxes heretofore lawfully assessed and due, or to become due, shall be collected pursuant to law, except as herein otherwise provided; but said Commissioners shall have no power to anticipate taxes by a sale or hypothecation of any such taxes or evidences thereof, but they may borrow, for the first fiscal year after this act takes effect, in anticipation of collection of revenues, not to exceed two hundred thousand dollars, at a rate of interest not exceeding five per centum, which shall be repaid out of the revenues of that year. And said Commissioners are hereby authorized to abolish any office, to consolidate two or more offices, reduce the number of employees, remove from office, and make appointments to any office under them authorized by law; said Commissioners shall have power to erect light, and maintain lampposts, with lamps, outside of the city limits, when, in their judgment, it shall be deemed proper or necessary: Provided, That nothing in this act contained shall be construed to abate in any wise or interfere with any suit pending in favor of or against the District of Columbia or the Commissioners thereof, or affect any right, penalty, forfeiture, or cause of action existing in favor of said District or Commissioners, or any citizen of the District of Columbia, or any other person, but the same may be commenced, proceeded for, or prosecuted to final judgment, and the corporation shall be bound thereby as if the suit had been originally commenced for or against said corporation. The said Commissioners shall submit to the Secretary of the Treasury for the fiscal year ending June thirtieth, eighteen hundred and seventy-nine, and annually thereafter, for his examination and approval, a statement showing in detail the work proposed to be undertaken by them during the fiscal year next ensuing, and the estimated cost thereof; also the cost of constructing, repairing, and maintaining all bridges authorized by law across the Potomac River within the District of Columbia, and also all other streams in said District; the cost of maintaining all public institutions of charity, reformatories, and prisons belonging to or controlled wholly or in part by the District of Columbia, and which are now by law supported wholly or in part by the United States or District of Columbia. . . .

PUBLIC IMPROVEMENTS FOR THE CAPITAL
1879

The provision of public improvements for the
city of Washington always caused difficulties
between the city's residents and Congress.
One of the most crucial improvements needed
was the draining and reclaiming of the city's
marshes. In 1879 President Rutherford B.
Hayes submitted a bill to Congress for these
purposes. What follows is his accompanying
message.

Source: James D. Richardson, comp. and ed., Messages and Papers of
the Presidents, X, New York, 1897.

EXECUTIVE MANSION,
December 19, 1879.

To the Senate and House of Representatives:

I have the honor to transmit herewith a draft of a bill submitted by the
Board of Commissioners of the District of Columbia, entitled "A bill to
provide for the reclamation of the marshes in the harbors of the cities of
Washington and Georgetown, and for other purposes," together with the
accompanying letter of the president of the board requesting its transmis-
sion to Congress.

The bill embraces a plan for the reclamation of the marshes of the Potomac River and its Eastern Branch within the limits of the city of Washington, and is carefully framed with a view to economy in the prosecution of
the work. The attention of Congress is again invited to the urgent need of
legislation for this important work, which has been so long delayed.

The improvement contemplated is essential to the health of those who
reside, whether permanently or temporarily, at the capital, and to the safe
and convenient navigation of the waters in its vicinity by vessels employed
in the service of the Government and for the purposes of commerce. It is
a measure of more than local benefit. The capital of the nation should be
relieved from every disadvantage which it is practicable to remove, and
should possess every attraction with which it can be invested by the intelligent and fostering care of those who are intrusted with its immediate supervision. The people of the country will sustain and approve the efforts of
their representatives in the discharge of this responsibility.

R. B. HAYES.

THE WASHINGTON MONUMENT
1885

One of the most distinctive landmarks of the
nation's capital is the Washington Monument.
Begun in 1848, construction of the massive
column took thirty-seven years as a result of
lack of funds, which halted its erection periodi-
cally. Finally, on February 22, 1885, the
monument was completed and dedicated. What
follows is a newspaper account of the dedication ceremonies.

Source: New York Times, February 22, 1885.

A rough board shed, bedecked with bunting, opening upon a snow-covered
field, and a simple towering shaft, greeted the eyes of those gathered in
the grand stand near the Washington Monument this morning. Despite the
cold, intensified by the sharp wind, the seats were quickly filled, among
the first comers being Ebenezer Barges Ball, of Loudoun County, Va. "I
am one of the Washington kindred," he said when asked for his ticket. "My
grandmother was George Washington's niece; my grandfather Ball was of
the family of Gen. Washington's mother, Mary Ball."

The military arrived, the bands were marshaled to their places, the
troops came to a rest, and then Senator Sherman, Chairman of the Joint
Congressional Committee, at 11 o'clock, called about 800 people to order,
and opened the proceedings with a brief address. "I need not say anything,"
he said, "to impress upon you the dignity of the event you have met to celebrate. The monument speaks for itself -- simple in form, admirable in
proportions, composed of enduring marble and granite, resting upon foun-
dations broad and deep, it rises into the skies higher than any other work
of human art. It is the most imposing, costly, and appropriate monument
ever erected in honor of one man. It had its origin in the profound conviction of the people, irrespective of party, creed, or race, not only of this
country, but of all civilized countries, that the name and fame of Washington should be perpetuated by the most imposing testimonial of a nation's
gratitude to its hero, statesman, and father. * * * It is a fit memorial of
the greatest character in human history. It looks down upon scenes most
loved by him on earth, the most conspicuous object in a landscape full of
objects deeply interesting to the American people. All eyes turn to it, and
all hearts feel the inspiration of its beauty, symmetry, and grandeur.
Strong as it is it will not endure so long as the memory of him in whose
honor it was built, but while it stands it will be the evidence to many succeeding generations of the love and reverence of this generation for the
name and fame of George Washington." . . .

THE PROCESSION.

Upon a signal from the Chairman, Senator Sherman, the assembly broke
into cheers. The military wheeled into line, the civic bodies and guests
sought their carriages, and the procession, under the marshalship of Gen.
Sheridan, took up its line of march. . . .

READING MR. WINTHROP'S ORATION.

From the hall of the House of Representatives the desks of the members
had been removed, and in their places were rows upon rows of chairs. The
seating capacity of the floor was about 1, 500. Early in the day the galleries
began to fill, and by 12 o'clock few vacant seats were to be found there.
The large majority of the spectators were ladies. The executive and diplomatic galleries were occupied, which is a very rare occurrence, and the
only vacant seats were in the gallery exclusively reserved for the families
of Senators and Representatives, and they became filled before the ceremonies began. Soon after 2 o'clock, when the House had signified its readi-
ness to begin the proceedings, the Washington Monument Society was announced. Soon afterward Gen. Sheridan and his staff entered, amid loud
clapping of hands, The President and his Cabinet next appeared, and the
large assemblage rose and heartily applauded. The Supreme Court, the
Judiciary of the District, and the diplomatic corps followed, and at 2:30
the Senate, preceded by its officers, was escorted to the space reserved for
it. Its presiding officer, Mr. Edmunds, proceeded to the Speaker's desk,
where the gavel was handed to him by Speaker Carlisle. In calling the assemblage to order Mr. Edmunds said:

GENTLEMEN: You are assembled pursuant to the concurrent order of
the two houses to celebrate the memorial occasion of the completion of the
monument to the memory of the first President of the United States. It is
not only a memorial but an inspiration that shall live through all the generations of our posterity, as we may hope, and which we this day inaugurate
and celebrate by ceremonies which have been ordered by the two houses.

Prayer was then offered by the Rev. T.A. Wallis, of Pohick church,
near Mount Vernon, Va.; the Marine Band played "Hail Columbia," and
then Representative John D. Long, of Massachusetts, read Mr. Winthrop's
oration. . . .

GEORGETOWN DISAPPEARS
1895

On February 11, 1895, Congress passed an act
by which the city of Georgetown was incorporated
into the city of Washington, becoming just another
section of the nation's capital. This act follows.

Source: District of Columbia Code, 1967 Ed., vol. I.

ACT OF 1895 CHANGING NAME OF GEORGETOWN

AN ACT Changing the name of Georgetown, in the District of Columbia, and
for other purposes

Be it enacted by the Senate and House of Representatives of the United
States of America in Congress assembled, That from and after the passage
of this act all that part of the District of Columbia embraced within the
bounds and now constituting the city of Georgetown, as referred to in said
acts of February twenty-first, eighteen hundred and seventy-one and June
twentieth, eighteen hundred and seventy-four, shall no longer be known by
the name and title in law of the city of Georgetown, but the same shall be
known as and shall constitute a part of the city of Washington, the Federal
Capital; and all general laws, ordinances, and regulations of the city of
Washington be, and the same are hereby, extended and made applicable to
that part of the District of Columbia formerly known as the city of Georgetown; and all general laws, regulations, and ordinances of the city of Georgetown be, and the same are hereby, repealed; that the title and existence of
said Georgetown as a separate and independent city by law is hereby abolished, and that the Commissioners of the District of Columbia be, and they
are hereby, directed to cause the nomenclature of the streets and avenues
of Georgetown to conform to those of Washington so far as practicable. And
the said Commissioners are also directed to have the squares in Georgetown renumbered, so that no square shall hereafter bear a like number to
any square in the city of Washington: Provided, That nothing in the Act shall
operate to affect or repeal existing law making Georgetown a port of entry,
except as to its name.

   Approved, February 11, 1895 (28 Stat. 650, ch. 79; see act of February
21, 1871, 16 Stat. 419, ch. 62, ante. p. 469.).

THE McMILLAN REPORT
1902

In January 1902, the Senate Park Commission
submitted its first official report. Senator
James McMillan, a member of the committee,
called for extensive changes in the entire layout
of the city. A portion of that report follows.

Source: U.S. Senate, District of Columbia Committee, 57th C., 1st 5,
The Improvement of the Park System of the District of Columbia, Washington, D.C., 1906.

The desirability of a comprehensive plan for the development of the District of Columbia has long been felt by Congress. During the past few years
particularly questions have arisen as to the location of public buildings, of
preserving spaces for parks in the portions of the District beyond the limits
of the city of Washington, of connecting and developing existing parks by at-
tractive drives, and of providing for the recreation and health of a constantly
growing population; and, in the absence of a well-considered plan, the solution of these grave problems has either been postponed or else has resulted
in compromises that have marred the beauty and dignity of the national capital.

I.

The action of the Senate in ordering a comprehensive plan for the development of the entire park system of the District of Columbia is the resultant
of two movements -- one popular in character, the other technical. In October, 1898, the citizens of the District of Columbia began to arrange for
the celebration, two years later, of the one hundredth anniversary of the
removal of the seat of government to the District of Columbia. The project,
being national in character rather than local, was brought to the attention
of the President, and by him was laid before Congress, with the result that
a joint committee of the two Houses was appointed to act with the citizen's
committee in planning the celebration. In December, 1900, commemorative
exercises, held at the White House and at the Capitol, were participated in
by the Governors of the States as well as by the officials of the General
Government and the representatives of foreign powers; and the celebration
was brought to an appropriate end by a reception and banquet given by the
Washington Board of Trade in honor of the Congressional committee and the
distinguished guests.

The keynote of the celebration was the improvement of the District of
Columbia in a manner and to an extent commensurate with the dignity and
the resources of the American nation. Senators and Congressmen vied with
Governor after Governor in commendation of the idea put forward by the

local committee, that the time had come for the systematic and adequate improvement of the District of Columbia.

While the centennial exercises were in progress the American Institute of Architects, in session in this city, was discussing the subject of improving Washington; and in a series of papers making suggestions for the development of parks and the placing of public buildings, the tentative ideas of a number of the leading architects, sculptors, and landscape architects of the country were put forward for discussion. As a result the Institute appointed a committee on legislation, and consultations between the committee and the Senate Committee on the District of Columbia were followed by the order of the Senate for the preparation and submission of a general plan for the development of the entire park system of the District.

II.

On March 19, 1901, the subcommittee of the District committee having the matter in charge met the representatives of the American Institute of Architects and agreed to the proposition of the latter that Mr. Daniel H. Burnham, of Chicago, Illinois, and Mr. Frederick Law Olmsted, jr., of Brookline, Massachusetts, be employed as experts, with power to add to their number. These gentlemen accepted the task, and subsequently invited Mr. Charles F. McKim and Mr. Augustus St. Gaudens, of New York City, to act with them in the preparation of plans. The committee considers itself most fortunate in having secured the services of men who had won the very highest places in their several professions.

As Director of Works at the World's Columbian Exposition, held in the city of Chicago in the year 1893, Mr. Burnham was instrumental in securing the adoption of a scheme of construction which placed that exhibition in the very front rank of international expositions; and by the display of rare executive ability he brought about and maintained the effective cooperation of the architects and artists who then and there gave to American art both a new direction and a tremendous impetus.

As the architect of the Boston Public Library, the Rhode Island capitol, the new buildings and the fence at Harvard University, and other structures of monumental character, Mr. McKim is recognized in his profession as without a superior among American architects, his work being especially notable for its simplicity, directness, and scholarly qualities.

Mr. St. Gaudens, by common consent, stands first among American sculptors; and among architects and artists his criticisms have the authority of law.

Mr. Olmsted bears a name identified with what is best in modern landscape architecture in the District of Columbia. He is the consulting landscape architect not only of the vast system of parks and boulevards which make up the metropolitan park system of Boston and its suburbs, but also of large parks in various cities. To inherited taste he adds the highest training, both practical and theoretical. . . .

PRESIDENT TAFT ON WASHINGTON
1910

Most of the presidents of the United States have
been concerned with the growth and development
of the nation's capital. William Howard Taft was
no exception. In 1910 he devoted a large portion
of his Second Annual Message to the city of Washington. Part of his report follows.

Source: James D. Richardson, comp. and ed., Messages and Papers of
the Presidents, XVI, New York, 1914.

CHARACTER OF GOVERNMENT.

The government of the District of Columbia is a good government. The
police force, while perhaps it might be given, or acquire, more military
discipline in bearing and appearance, is nevertheless an efficient body of
men, free from graft, and discharges its important duties in this capital
of the nation effectively. The parks and the streets of the city and the District
are generally kept clean and in excellent condition. The Commissioners
of the District have its affairs well in hand, and, while not extravagant, are
constantly looking to those municipal improvements that are expensive but
that must be made in a modern growing city like Washington. While all
this is true, nevertheless the fact that Washington is governed by Congress,
and that the citizens are not responsible and have no direct control through
popular election in District matters, properly subjects the government to
inquiry and criticism by its citizens, manifested through the public press
and otherwise; such criticism should command the careful attention of Congress. Washington is the capital of the nation and its maintenance as a
great and beautiful city under national control, every lover of his country
has much at heart; and it should present in every way a model in respect of
economy of expenditure, of sanitation, of tenement reform, of thorough public instruction, of the proper regulation of public utilities, or sensible and
extended charities, of the proper care of criminals and of youth needing reform, of healthful playgrounds and opportunity for popular recreation, and
of a beautiful system of parks. I am glad to think that progress is being
made in all these directions, but I venture to point out certain improvements
toward these ends which Congress in its wisdom might adopt. Speaking
generally, I think there ought to be more concentration of authority in respect to the accomplishment of some of these purposes with more economy
of expenditure.

PUBLIC PARKS.

Attention is invited to the peculiar situation existing in regard to the
parks of Washington. The park system proper, comprising some 343 dif-

ferent areas, is under the Office of Public Buildings and Grounds, which, however, has nothing to do with the control of Rock Creek Park, the Zoological Park, the grounds of the Department of Agriculture, the Botanic Garden, the grounds of the Capitol, and other public grounds which are regularly open to the public and ought to be part of the park system. Exclusive of the grounds of the Soldiers' Home and of Washington Barracks, the public grounds used as parks in the District of Columbia comprise over 3,100 acres, under ten different controlling officials or bodies. This division of jurisdiction is most unfortunate.

Large sums of money are spent yearly in beautifying and keeping in good condition these parks and the grounds connected with Government buildings and institutions. The work done on all of them is of the same general character -- work for which the Office of Public Buildings and Grounds has been provided by Congress with a special organization and equipment, which are lacking for the grounds not under that office. There can be no doubt that if all work of care and improvement upon the grounds belonging to the United States in the District of Columbia were put, as far as possible, under one responsible head, the result would be not only greater efficiency and economy in the work itself, but greater harmony in the development of the public parks and gardens of the city.

Congress at its last session provided for two more parks, called the Meridian Hill and Montrose parks, and the District Commissioners have also included in their estimates a sum to be used for the acquisition of much needed park land adjoining the Zoological Park, known as the Klingle Ford tract. The expense of these three parks, included in the estimates of the Commissioners, aggregates $900,000. I think it would lead to economy if the improvement and care of all these parks and other public grounds above described should be transferred to the Office of Public Buildings and Grounds, which has an equipment well and economically adapted to carrying out the public purpose in respect to improvements of this kind.

To prevent encroachments upon the park area it is recommended that the erection of any permanent structure on any lands in the District of Columbia belonging to the United States be prohibited except by specific authority of Congress. . . .

THE ALLEY DWELLING ACT
1914

> Congress passed an act which was designed to
> convert the most notorious alleys in the city into
> streets or parks. It also prohibited the construc-
> tion of any type of housing in the alleys of the
> District of Columbia. This act follows.

Source: U.S. Laws and Statutes, U.S. Laws at Large, Vol. 38, part I,
Washington, D.C., 1913-1915.

Be it enacted by the Senate and House of Representatives of the United
States of America in Congress assembled, That from and after the passage
of this Act it shall be unlawful in the District of Columbia to erect, place,
or construct any dwelling on any lot or parcel of ground fronting on an alley
where such alley is less than thirty feet wide throughout its entire length
and which does not run straight to and open on two of the streets bordering
the square, and is not supplied with sewer, water mains, and gas or electric light; and in this Act the term "alley" shall include any and all courts,
passages, and thoroughfares, whether public or private, and any ground
intended for or used as a highway other than the public streets or avenues;
and any dwelling house now fronting an alley less than thirty feet wide and
not extending straight to the streets and provided with sewer, water main,
and light, as aforesaid, which has depreciated or been damaged more than
one-half its original value, shall not be repaired or reconstructed as a
dwelling or for use as such, and no permit shall be issued for the alteration,
repair, or reconstruction of such a building, when the plans indicate any
provision for dwelling purposes: Provided, That rooms for grooms or sta-
blemen to be employed in the building to be erected, repaired, or reconstructed may be allowed over stables, when the means of exit and safeguards against fire are sufficient, in the opinion of the inspector of buildings, subject to the approval of the Commissioners of the District of Columbia; and no building now or hereafter erected fronting on an alley or on any
parcel of ground fronting on an alley less than thirty feet wide and not otherwise in accordance with this Act shall be altered or converted to the uses
of a dwelling. Any such alley house depreciated or damaged more than one-
half of its original value shall be condemned as provided by law for the removal of dangerous or unsafe buildings and part thereof, and for other purposes. No dwelling house hereafter erected or placed along any alley and
fronting or facing thereon shall in any case be located less than twenty feet
back clear of the center line of such alley, so as to give at least thirty-foot
roadway and five feet on each side of such roadway clear for a walk or footway, and any stable or other building hereafter placed, located, altered, or

erected on or along such an alley upon which a dwelling faces or fronts shall be set back clear of the walk or footway the same as the dwellings, but the fact that dwellings are located in such alleys shall not affect the location of stables or other buildings otherwise.

The use or occupation of any building or other structure erected or placed on or along any such alley as a dwelling or residence or place of abode by any person or persons is hereby declared injurious to life, to public health, morals, safety, and welfare of said District; and such use or occupation of any such building or other structure on, from, and after the first day of July, nineteen hundred and eighteen, shall be unlawful.

SEC. 2. That any person or persons, whether as principal, agent, or employee, violating any of the provisions of this Act or any amendment thereof for the violation of which no other penalty is prescribed, shall on conviction thereof in the police court, be punished by a fine of not less than $10 nor more than $100 for each such violation, and a like fine for each day during which such violation has continued or may continue, to be recovered as other fines and penalties are recovered.

SEC. 3. That the Act of Congress approved July twenty-second, eighteen hundred and ninety-two, entitled "An Act regulating the construction of buildings along alleyways in the District of Columbia," and all laws or parts of laws inconsistent with the provisions hereof, are hereby repealed.

RIOT IN WASHINGTON
1919

Caused by racial tensions and fears engendered by
radical actions in the wake of the spread of Communism in Europe, Washington exploded into a full
scale race riot for five stormy days in July 1919.
A description of the riot is provided by the following
selection.

Source: New York Times, July 21, 1919.

WASHINGTON, Monday, July 21. -- Police reserves were called out
last night because of rioting in the Centre Market district, Seventh and
Pennsylvania Avenue, in the very heart of the city, to quell soldiers, sailors, marines, and civilians who made attacks on negroes in retalliation for
attacks on white women in Washington during the past month.

Several hundred soldiers, sailors, and marines participated in the rioting, along with more than a thousand civilians. Negroes were hauled
from street cars and from automobiles. The Provost Guard was called out,
and at 10:20 the police reserves.

Half a dozen arrests were made. Among those taken into custody were
a sailor and a soldier. They were charged with disorderly conduct.

Attack Near White House.

Reports were received by the police of attacks late at night on negroes
in several parts of the city, and the belief was expressed that these were
the result of organized action.

Late at night several negroes were attacked by soldiers and marines
at Fifteenth Street and New York Avenue Northwest, near the Riggs National
Bank and within a stone's throw of the White House. Three negroes beaten
here were taken to the Third Precinct Police Station.

A band of soldiers and sailors dragged a young negro from a street car
on G Street, Northwest, between Ninth and Tenth streets. They beat him
and chased him several blocks. His head was cut. He was taken home by
the police.

At 1 o'clock this morning a riot call was sent in to police headquarters
from Ninth Street and New York Avenue. All available reserves were sent
there in patrol wagons under command of Captain Flaherty.

It was reported that from 200 to 250 soldiers, sailors, and marines
were engaged in an attack there on negroes.

A second riot call was sent in from Tenth and L Streets, N.W., at 1:05
A.M. A patrol wagon loaded with policemen was sent out. This place is
about three blocks from Ninth Street and New York Avenue.

The group of soldiers responsible for most of the attacks moved into the Second Precinct, where they attacked negroes near the American League baseball park and drew the reserves of that precinct into action. At 2:15 o'clock the city was quiet, but reserves were still on duty.

A late report puts the number of negroes taken to the Emergency Hospital from various parts of the city at fifteen. One of the men who was attacked in the Seventh Street riot had his collarbone broken. A number of negroes who were brought bruised and bleeding into police stations were badly frightened and refused to go to their homes except under police escort.

Policeman Hellmuth, who arrested a soldier near Seventh Street and Pennsylvania Avenue, N.W., shortly after 11 o'clock, was threatened by a large crowd of soldiers, sailors, and civilians. He fought off the crowd, but finally was forced to draw his revolver and fire into the air. He managed to hold his prisoner until the patrol wagon arrived.

A number of disturbances were caused by civilians who, when a crowd of soldiers and sailors collected, pointed to any negro who might be passing and yelled, "There he goes!" Such outcries generally were followed by an attack upon the negro by some of the sailors and soldiers.

All of the policemen who reported off duty at midnight were ordered to sections where the attacks had occurred, with instructions to remain on duty until further orders.

The rioting was a repetition of disorders late Saturday night and early Sunday morning, when two hundred soldiers, sailors, and marines bent on lynching a negro in connection with an attack on a white woman in Southwest Washington forced the police to call out the reserves.

Calling out of the reserves two nights in a row for rioting is something that has not occurred in Washington since the days, many years ago, shortly after the Civil War, when there were riots during the period of the old "Feather Duster Legislature" which met before the present form of Government was organized.

Women Attacked in Suburbs.

The activity of the men in uniform Saturday night was precipitated by the latest of a series of attacks on white women by negroes in Washington. During the last month there have been many of these attacks. Most of them have taken place in the northwestern suburbs, and some of the women attacked have been girls who came to Washington for employment as war workers. The Police Department has been active in trying to run down the assailants, and, while arrests have been made, the real assailants are believed to be still at large.

As a result of the rioting Saturday night and early Sunday morning in the southwest section of Washington ten arrests were made by the police. During this outbreak Policeman Frank C. McGrath of the Fourth Precinct was shot in the breast and seriously wounded and a bullet was fired at Policeman Cox. Two negroes were beaten with clubs and a dozen others were seriously injured. . . .

NATIONAL CAPITAL PARK AND PLANNING COMMISSION
1926

In 1926 Congress created the National Capital Park
and Planning Commission, whose purpose was to see
to the improvement of the city of Washington. Some
of the sections of the act follow.

Source: District of Columbia, Laws and Statutes, The Code of the District
of Columbia to March 4, 1929, Washington, D.C. 1930.

Section 1531. Park and playground system; National Capital Park and
Planning Commission --
  (a) Establishment of commission; composition; term; compensation
and expenses; executive and disbursing officer. -- To develop a comprehensive, consistent, and coordinated plan for the National Capital and its
environs in the States of Maryland and Virginia, to preserve the flow of
water in Rock Creek, to prevent pollution of Rock Creek and the Potomac
and Anacostia Rivers, to preserve forests and natural scenery in an about
Washington, and to provide for the comprehensive, systematic, and continuous development of park, parkway, and playground systems of the National Capital and its environs there is hereby constituted a commission to
be known as the National Capital Park and Planning Commission, composed
of the Chief of Engineers of the Army, the Engineer Commissioner of the
District of Columbia, the Director of the National Park Service, the Chief
of the Forest Service, the Director of Public Buildings and Public Parks of
the National Capital, the chairmen of the Committees on the District of Columbia of the Senate and House of Representatives, and four eminent citizens well qualified and experienced in city planning, one of whom shall be
a bona fide resident of the District of Columbia, to be appointed for the
term of six years by the President of the United States: Provided, That the
first members appointed under this section shall continue in office for terms
of three, four, five, and six years, respectively, from April 30, 1926, the
terms of each to be designated by the President; but their successors shall
be appointed for terms of six years, except that any person chosen to fill
a vacancy shall be appointed only for the unexpired term of the member
whom he shall succeed. All members of the said commission shall serve
without compensation therefor, but each shall be paid actual expenses of
travel when attending meetings of said commission or engaged in investiga-
tions pertaining to its activities, and an allowance of $8 per day in lieu of
subsistence during such travel and services. At the close of each Congress
the presiding officer of the Senate and the Speaker of the House of Representatives shall appoint, respectively, a Senator and a Representative elect
to the succeeding Congress to serve as members of this commission until

the chairman of the committees of the succeeding Congress shall be chosen. The Director of Public Buildings and Public Parks of the National Capital shall be executive and disbursing officer of said commission.

(b) Duties; employment of personal services and experts. -- That the said commission is hereby charged with the duty of preparing, developing, and maintaining a comprehensive, consistent, and coordinated plan for the National Capital and its environs, which plan shall include recommendations to the proper executive authorities as to traffic and transportation; plats and subdivisions; highways, parks, and parkways; school and library sites; playgrounds; drainage, sewerage, and water supply; housing, building, and zoning regulations; public and private buildings; bridges and water fronts; commerce and industry; and other proper elements of city and regional planning. It is the purpose of this section to obtain the maximum amount of cooperation and correlation of effort between the departments, bureaus, and commissions of the Federal and District Governments. To this end plans and records, or copies thereof, shall be made available to the National Capital Park and Planning Commission, when requested. The commission may, as to the environs of the District of Columbia, act in conjunction and cooperation with such representatives of the States of Maryland and Virginia as may be designated by such States for this purpose. The said commission is hereby authorized to employ the necessary personal services, including the personal services of a director of planning and other expert city planners, such as engineers, architects, and landscape architects. Such technical experts may be employed at per diem rates not in excess of those paid for similar services elsewhere and as may be fixed by the said commission without regard to the provisions of sections 661 and 674 of Title 5 of the Code of the Laws of the United States or any rule or regulation made in pursuance thereof.

(c) Authorities and duties of National Park Commission transferred. -- All authority, powers, and duties conferred and imposed by law on the National Capital Park Commission shall after April 30, 1926, be held, exercised, and performed by the National Capital Park and Planning Commission hereby constituted. All appropriations heretofore made for expenditure by the National Capital Park Commission are hereby made available for the use of the commission hereby constituted. (Apr. 30, 1926, 44 Stat. 374, c. 198.). . . .

THE BONUS ARMY
1932

In July 1932, about 7, 000 veterans arrived in
Washington to demand that Congress immediately cash, in full, the adjusted compensation
certificates they had been given after the end
of World War I. They were known as the "Bonus
Army." They camped on the Anacostia Flats,
on the edge of the city. When Congress refused
their request, many of them went home, but
about 2, 000 of them squatted in the capital, refusing to disband. Violence broke out when
Washington police attempted to evict them.
Troops were called in to complete the removal.
The following selections are a description of
the fighting between the veterans and the troops,
and President Hoover's statement on calling
out the army to end the "Bonus Army" rioting.

Source: New York Times, July 29, 1932; Government Printing Office, The
Public Papers of the Presidents: Herbert Hoover, 1929-1933, 4 vols.,
Washington, D.C., 1936.

WASHINGTON, July 28. -- Amidst scenes reminiscent of the mopping-
up of a town in the World War, Federal troops late today drove the army of
bonus seekers from the shanty village near Pennsylvania Avenue in which
the veterans had been entrenched for months. Earlier in the day the police
had fought and lost a battle there which resulted in the death of one veteran,
possibly fatal injuries to a policeman and a long list of other casualties,
many of them serious.

Ordered to the scene by President Hoover after the District of Columbia
authorities confessed defeat, detachments of infantry, cavalry, machine-
gun and tank crews laid down an effective tear-gas barrage which diorgan-
ized the bonus-seekers, and then set fire to the shacks and tents left behind
by the veterans on the government land near Third and Pennsylvania Avenues,
scene of the earlier clash with the police.

Begin to Clear Anacostia.

After the disputed area near the Capitol had been cleared, the troops
moved late in the evening on Camp Marks, on the Anacostia River, the bonus army's principal encampment. At 10 o'clock this evening infantrymen
with drawn bayonets advanced into the camp, driving the crowd before them
with tear gas bombs. Then they applied the torch to the shacks in which
the veterans lived.

Troops shortly afterward halted at the main bonus camp in response to what General Perry L. Miles, commanding the soldiers, said was a Presidential order. Theodore G. Joslin, the President's secretary, later denied positively that the President had issued any such order, and word came from the camp that the troops would resume operations within an hour.

At 11:15 P.M. the first troop of cavalry had moved into the disordered camp, now a mass of flames as the bonus-seeking veterans set fire to their own miserable shacks. At midnight practically all the veterans had left the place.

Warned that the soldiers would use tear gas the veterans had arranged to evacuate the 600 women and children earlier.

The normal population of Camp Marks was augmented by more than 2,000 veterans who had been evicted from other camps, bringing the total male population to 7,000.

Troops Avoid Bloodshed.

Soon after the khaki-clad regulars descended on the various camps along Pennsylvania Avenue this afternoon the bonus seekers were straggling sullenly away from the ominous blue mist of the tear gas, leaderless and apparently demoralized, seeking shelter in other open places scattered afar through the city. A few of them were sore from minor bruises, but on the whole the Federal troops had conducted their offensive without bloodshed. The veteran who was killed in the earlier clash with the police was identified tonight as William Hashka of Chicago.

The day's distrubances were blamed on the radical element among the bonus-seekers. Walter W. Waters, the young veteran from Oregon who led the unsuccessful bonus march to Washington, disclaimed responsibility for his followers' part in resisting the first eviction order of the police. Waters announced tonight that he was "through."

"The men got out of control. There was nothing and there is nothing that I can do to control them," he said. . . .

Flames rose high over the desolate Anacostia flats at midnight tonight and a pitiful stream of refugee veterans of the World War walked out of their home of the past two months, going they knew not where.

Cavalry stood guard at all the bridges leading across the river to the camp and thousands of onlookers gazed across the river at what had been the teeming residence of 20,000 persons.

The veterans were leaving at the behest of the military forces of the government, summoned by the President after collisions between the bonus marchers and the police. Some were departing in broken-down automobiles; some, on foot, dragged listlessly in search of new quarters.

Flames were raging in the camp. Many of the tents, numbering 2,100 and mostly belonging to the army, were ablaze and the infantry was busy trying to salvage as many as possible.

A heavy barrage of tear gas, laid down by the troops, penetrated to the houses for blocks around, and residents were forced to close their doors and windows in spite of the sweltering heat.

Had Thirty Minutes to Evacuate.

It was soon after 9 o'clock tonight that the troops, headed by General MacArthur, surrounded the main camp of the Bonus Expeditionary force at Anacostia, wheeled their ranks into position, unlimbered their bombs and gave the thousands of veterans massed there thirty minutes in which to evacuate. . . . Walter W. Waters, titular commander of the "Bonus Expeditionary Force," declared tonight that "no matter what may happen from now on, the B.E.F. will carry on."

"If driven from Washington, it will organize elsewhere and continue the fight for justice for the veterans and the common people of the United States" he said in a statement. "We have gone too far now to quit."

The Waters declaration, telephoned to newspaper offices, included the assertion that a life was sacrificed "to serve the political interests of the administration."

The one-time dictator of the bonus army watched from the sidelines while the men who formerly paid him allegiance swept completely out of his control

Before Federal troops arrived to push former service men off their encampments in front of a cloud of tear gas, "Commander" Waters threw up his hands in a gesture of defeat. He said frankly that he no longer had any control over the men.

Accompanied by a handful of his aides, Waters viewed from the sidewalks about the trouble-ridden area the swiftly breaking developments, which resulted in the death of a war veteran. . . .

PRESIDENT HOOVER'S STATEMENT

For some days police authorities and Treasury officials have been endeavoring to persuade the so-called bonus marchers to evacuate certain buildings which they were occupying without permission.

These buildings are on sites where government construction is in progress and their demolition was necessary in order to extend employment in the district and to carry forward the government's construction program.

This morning the occupants of these buildings were notified to evacuate and at the request of the police did evacuate the buildings concerned. Thereafter, however, several thousand men from different camps marched in and attacked the police with brickbats and otherwise injuring several policemen, one probably fatally.

I have received the attached letter from the Commissioners of the District of Columbia, stating that they can no longer preserve law and order in the district.

In order to put an end to this rioting and defiance of civil authority, I have asked the army to assist the District authorities to restore order.

Congress made provision for the return home of the so-called bonus marchers, who have for many weeks been given every opportunity of free assembly, free speech and free petition to the Congress. Some 5,000 took advantage of this arrangement and have returned to their homes. An examination of a large number of names discloses the fact that a considerable part of those remaining are not veterans; many are Communists and persons with criminal records.

The veterans amongst these numbers are no doubt unaware of the character of their companions and are being led into violence which no government can tolerate.

I have asked the Attorney General to investigate the whole incident and to cooperate with the District civil authorities in such measures against leaders and rioters as may be necessary.

THE SCHOOL APPROPRIATION ACT
1936

Although the city of Washington, like the rest of
the nation, was experiencing difficult times during the great depression of the 1930s, Congress
passed a relatively generous appropriation act for
the city's public schools. It also attached the "Red
Rider" clause, which denied salary to any Washington teacher who taught the principles of communism
in his classroom.

Source: United States Statutes at Large, vol. 49, pp. 353-357.

PUBLIC SCHOOLS

For personal services of administrative and supervisory officers in
accordance with the Act fixing and regulating the salaries of teachers,
school officers, and other employees of the Board of Education of the District of Columbia, approved June 4, 1924 (re Stat., pp. 367-375), including salaries of presidents of teachers colleges in the salary schedule for
first assistant superintendents, $671,100.

For personal services of clerks and other employees, $187,880.

For personal services in the department of school attendance and work
permits in accordance with the Act approved June 4, 1924 (43 Stat., pp.
367-375), the Act approved February 5, 1925 (43 Stat., pp. 806-808), and
the Act approved May 29, 1923 (45 Stat., p. 998), $41,900.

For personal services of teachers and librarians in accordance with
the Act approved June 4, 1924 (43 Stat., pp. 367-375), including for teachers
colleges assistant professors in salary class eleven, and professors in salary class twelve, $6,953,100, of which not exceeding $5,000 may be expended for compensation to be fixed by the Board of Education and traveling expenses of educational consultants employed on special educational projects:
Provided, That as teacher vacancies occur during the fiscal year 1936 in
grades one to four, inclusive, of the elementary schools, such vacancies
may be filled by the assignment of teachers now employed in kindergartens,
and teachers employed in kindergartens are hereby made eligible to teach
in the said grades: Provided further, That teaching vacancies that occur
during the fiscal year 1936 wherever found may be filled by the assignment
of teachers of special subjects and teachers not now assigned to classroom
instruction, and such teachers are hereby made eligible for such assignment without further examination.

For the instruction and supervision of children in the vacation schools
and playgrounds, and supervisors and teachers of vacation schools and play-

playgrounds may also be supervisors and teachers of day schools, $29,400.

No part of any appropriation made in this Act shall be paid to any person employed under or in connection with the public schools of the District of Columbia who shall solicit or receive, or permit to be solicited or received, on any public-school premises, any subscription or donation of money or other thing of value from any pupil enrolled in such public schools for presentation of testimonials to school officials or for any purpose except such as may be authorized by the Board of Education at a stated meeting upon the written recommendation of the superintendent of schools.

To carry out the purposes of the Act approved June 11, 1926, entitled "An Act to amend the Act entitled 'An Act for the retirement of public-school teachers in the District of Columbia', approved January 15, 1920, and for other purposes" (41 Stat., pp.387-390), $400,000.

NIGHT SCHOOLS

For teachers and janitors of night schools, including teachers of industrial, commercial, and trade instruction, and teachers and janitors of night schools may also be teachers and janitors of day schools, $91,360.

For contingent and other necessary expenses, including equipment and purchase of all necessary articles and supplies for classes in industrial, commercial, and trade instruction, $10,000.

THE DEAF, DUMB, AND BLIND

For maintenance and instruction of deaf and dumb persons admitted to the Columbia Institution for the Deaf from the District of Columbia, under section 4864 of the Revised Statutes, and as provided for in the Act approved March 1, 1901 (U.S.C., title 24, sec. 238), and under a contract to be entered into with the said institution by the Commissioners, $34,500.

For maintenance and instruction of colored deaf-mutes of teachable age belonging to the District of Columbia, in Maryland, or some other State, under a contract to be entered into by the Commissioners, $5,000: Provided, That all expenditures under this appropriation shall be made under the supervision of the Board of Education.

For maintenance and instruction of blind children of the District of Columbia, in Maryland, or some other State, under a contract to be entered into by the Commissioners, $11,500: Provided, That all expenditures under this appropriation shall be made under the supervision of the Board of Education.

AMERICANIZATION WORK

For Americanization work and instruction of foreigners of all ages in both day and night classes, and teachers and janitors of Americanization schools may also be teachers and janitors of the day schools, $8,800.

For contingent and other necessary expenses, including books, equipment, and supplies, $600.

For carrying out the provisions of the Act of June 19, 1934 (48 Stat., p. 1125), entitled "An Act providing educational opportunities for the children of soldiers, sailors, and marines who were killed in action or died during the World War", $3,000.

COMMUNITY CENTER DEPARTMENT

For personal services of the director, general secretaries, and community secretaries in accordance with the Act approved June 4, 1924 (43 Stat., pp. 369, 370); clerks and part-time employees, including janitors on account of meetings of parent-teacher associations and other activities, and contingent expenses, equipment, supplies, and lighting fixtures, $50,000.

CARE OF BUILDINGS AND GROUNDS

For personal services, including care of smaller buildings and rented rooms at a rate not to exceed $96 per annum for the care of each schoolroom, other than those occupied by atypical or ungraded classes, for which service an amount not to exceed $120 per annum may be allowed, $915,360.
. . .

The children of officers and men of the United States Army, Navy and Marine Corps, and children of other employees of the United States stationed outside the District of Columbia shall be admitted to the public schools without payment of tuition: [Provided, That hereafter no part of any appropriation for the public schools shall be available for the payment of the salary of any person teaching or advocating Communism.]   Red Rider Clause.

For repairs and improvements to school buildings and grounds, repairing and renewing heating, plumbing, and ventilating apparatus, installation and repair of electric equipment, and installation of sanitary drinking fountains, and maintenance of motor trucks, including not to exceed $1,950 for the purchase of two one and one-half ton trucks, $420,950, of which amount $100,000 shall be immediately available.

For the purchase, installation, and maintenance of equipment, for school yards for the purposes of play of pupils, $7,000: Provided, That such playgrounds shall be kept open for play purposes in accordance with the schedule maintained for playgrounds under the jurisdiction of the playground department.

BUILDINGS AND GROUNDS

For the construction of an eight-room building on the old John F. Cook School site, $110,000.

For the construction of an addition to the Eliot Junior High School, including ten classrooms and one gymnasium, $175,000.

For the construction of an eight-room addition to the Randall Junior High School, including remodeling of the present heating plant, $100,000.

For beginning construction of an addition to the Anacostia Junior High School to be used for senior high school pupils, $250,000, and the Commissioners are authorized to enter into contract or contracts for said construction at a cost not to exceed $350,000.

For the completion of construction, and for improvement of grounds of the Woodrow Wilson High School, $70,000.

For the purchase of additional land at the Phelps Vocational School for elementary-school purposes, $55,000.

In all, $830,000 to be immediately available and to be disbursed. . . .

THE REDEVELOPMENT ACT
1945

Congress passed a redevelopment act for Washington. It vested in the National Capital Park and
Planning Commission authority to plan the rebuilding of all of the city's slum areas, to lay out a new
highway system, to specify sites for new public
buildings, and to purchase land for new parks and
playgrounds. A portion of the act follows.

Source: District of Columbia, Laws and Statutes, Acts of Congress Affecting the District of Columbia passed by the 79th Congress, vol. 45, Washington, D.C., 1946.

Be it enacted by the Senate and House of Representatives of the United
States of America in Congress assembled, That this Act may be cited as
the "District of Columbia Redevelopment Act of 1945".
GENERAL PURPOSES
SEC. 2. It is hereby declared to be a matter of legislative determination that owing to technological and sociological changes, obsolete lay-out,
and other factors, conditions existing in the District of Columbia with respect to substandard housing and blighted areas, including the use of buildings in alleys as dwellings for human habitation, are injurious to the public
health, safety, morals, and welfare, and it is hereby declared to be the
policy of the United States to protect and promote the welfare of the inhabitants of the seat of the Government by eliminating all such injurious conditions by employing all means necessary and appropriate for the purpose;
and control by regulatory processes having proved inadequate and insuffi-
cient to remedy the evils, it is in the judgment of Congress necessary to
acquire property in the District of Columbia by gift, purchase, or the use
of eminent domain to effectuate the declared policy by the discontinuance
of the use for human habitation in the District of Columbia of substandard
dwellings and of buildings in alleys and blighted areas, and thereby to eli-
minate the substandard housing conditions and the communities in the inhabited alleys and blighted areas in such District; and it is necessary to mo-
dernize the planning and development of such portions of such District.
The Congress finds that the foregoing cannot be accomplished by the ordinary operations of private enterprise alone without public participation in
the planning and in the financing of land assembly for such development;
and that for the economic soundness of this redevelopment and the accomplishment of the necessary social and economic benefits, and by reason of
any part of an urban area with the development and uses of all other parts
the sound replanning and redevelopment of an obsolescent or obsolescing

portion of such District cannot be accomplished unless it be done in the light of comprehensive and coordinated planning of the whole of the territory of the District of Columbia and its environs; and that this comprehensive planning and replanning should proceed vigorously without delay; and to these ends it is necessary to enact the provisions hereinafter set forth; and that the acquisition and the assembly of real property and the leasing or sale thereof for redevelopment pursuant to a project area redevelopment plan, all as provided in this Act, is hereby declared to be a public use. . . .

THE STRAYER REPORT
1949

George Strayer of Columbia University was com-
missioned by Congress to undertake a survey of
Washington's public school system. His report
was highly critical of a number of deficiencies in
the city's education setup. A portion of the report
follows.

Source: George D. Strayer, The Report of a Survey of the Public Schools
of the District of Columbia, Washington, 1949.

The administration of the school system of the District of Columbia
presents unique problems. The fact that the government of the District is
a matter of immediate congressional control indicates at once the unusual
relationships through which the educational administration must function.
With no governmental arrangement through which citizens of the District
can register their approval or disapproval of prevailing educational policies,
administrative authorities should be unusually sensitive to the reasonable
concern among civic groups for improved educational service.

It is necessary to interpret and evaluate the administrative organization of any community through the peculiarity of its traditional background,
and no less through the constant effort which should have been made to meet
ever changing educational needs. To the extent that the administrative program is responsive to changing social and civic needs it tends to insure in-
creasingly effective instructional services. To the extent that the administrative organization has a tendency to become inflexible, or to hold to out-
worn traditional procedures, it must be called a question.

In the study which follows covering the administrative policies and procedures of the local school organization the principle is accepted as funda-
mental that school administration should be democratic rather than authori-
tarian. As a general rule, the more immediate the responsibility of the
school administrator to the influence of public opinion, the greater the probability of a reasonable degree of democratization in the administrative and
supervisory services.

The function of a board of education, the relation of a board to their
executive officer, the superintendent of schools; his relationship in turn to
the administrative and supervisory staff, and through the staff to principals
and teachers, are all vital issues involved in the interpretation of the administrative procedures. More than rules or regulations, these matters
become problems in human relations. In the final analysis efficient school
administration has no other function than to serve in the highest possible degree every phase of the educational program.

Under wise and efficient administrative direction and with adequate fi-

nancial support the school system of the District of Columbia should illus-
trate the highest possible standards of educational practice and achievement.
An efficient organization must be based upon sound administrative principles.
This is as important in educational administration as in the managerial or
supervisory service of business corporations. It is even more important
because of the human factor. To the extent that the administrative organization serves the instructional program, democratically and cooperatively,
to that degree is educational administration effective.

BOARD OF EDUCATION

In any evaluation of the administrative organization of the school system of the District of Columbia it is necessary to interpret the functions of
the Board of Education and of the school administrative organization through
the District Code relating to the government of the District and more speci-
fically through those sections known as title 31, Educational and Cultural
Institutions.

Unique character of the District school system

The Board of Education is the highest educational authority for the
school system in the District. In the formulation of the policies, in the development and improvement of the schools, the Board of Education has supreme control, subject only to the acts of the Congress. In this respect the
school system of the District of Columbia is unique. In every State, and
therefore in every city of the Nation, a local board of education operates
under the general framework of a State educational plan. Such a board of
education is also subject to the State education authority. In the District
of Columbia, however, the legislative mandate for "the control of the public schools" by the Board of Education comes direct from the Congress.

> The control of the public schools of the District of Columbia
> is hereby vested in a Board of Education to consist of nine
> members all of whom shall have been for five years imme-
> diately preceding their appointment bona fide residents of
> the District of Columbia and three of whom shall be women.
> The members of the Board of Education shall be appointed
> by the District court judges of the District of Columbia for
> terms of three years each, and members shall be eligible
> for reappointment. The members shall serve without com-
> pensation. Vacancies for unexpired terms, caused by death,
> resignation, or otherwise, shall be filled by the judges of
> the District Court of the United States for the District of Co-
> lumbia. The Board shall appoint a secretary, who shall not
> be a member of the Board, and they shall hold stated meet-
> ings at least once a month during the school year and such
> additional meetings as they shall from time to time provide
> for. All meetings whatsoever of the Board shall be open to
> the public, except committee meetings dealing with the ap-
> pointment of teachers. (31-101)

As may be noted above the members of the Board of Education are ap-

pointed by the District court judges of the District of Columbia. These
judges are appointed by the President of the United States. The citizens of
the District therefore have no voice in the selection of the Board of Education, neither do they have any control even indirectly in the educational of-
ferings provided for their children. The schools of the District are under
the control of the Board of Education, and the Board of Education is immediately responsible to the Federal Government.

> The board shall determine all questions of general policy re-
> lating to the schools, shall appoint the executive officers
> hereinafter provided for, define their duties, and direct ex-
> penditures. All expenditures of public funds for such school
> purposes shall be made and accounted for as provided in sec-
> tion 47-101, under the direction and control of the commis-
> sioners of the District of Columbia. The board shall appoint
> all teachers in the manner hereinafter prescribed and all
> other employees provided for in this chapter. (31-103)

The independence of the Board of Education in educational matters does
not obtain in financial matters. Expenditures may be made only "under the
direction and control of the Commissioners of the District of Columbia."
The Commissioners, three in number, constitute the governing body of the
District. In one sense therefore, the development of the educational program is limited to such budgetary support as may receive the approval of
the District Commissioners. Budgetary estimates after approval by the
District Committees, to the congressional Appropriations Committees, and
the appropriations finally made available by congressional act.

> The Board of Education shall annually on the first day of Oc-
> tober transmit to the commissioners of the District of Co-
> lumbia an estimate in detail of the amount of money required
> for the public schools for the ensuring year, and said com-
> missioners shall transmit the same in their annual estimate
> of appropriations for the District of Columbia, with such re-
> commendations as they may deem proper. (31-104)

The Board of Education exercises independent control of the school system in all matters except those which have to do directly with finance. The
construction and maintenance of school buildings, pursuant to this policy,
are under the control of the Commissioners of the District of Columbia.
But the care of school buildings is under the direction of the Board of Education. This conflict of control which obtains in connection with the submission of the budgetary estimates in some degree extends into all expenditures for educational purposes.

The enabling act states that "the Board shall determine all questions
of general policy relating to the schools," and "shall appoint the executive
officers hereinafter provided for." This emphasis on the function of the
Board in the determination of matters of "general policy" is in full accord
with sound educational administration. However, under the committee system, as it operates at present, the Board of Education finds its calendar
congested more and more with matters of administrative routine. . . .

WASHINGTON'S METROPOLITAN PROBLEMS -- 1958

By 1958, the Washington Metropolitan area had grown to very
large proportions. A Joint Committee on Washington Metropolitan Problems began studying the growth and expansion of the
District of Columbia's Metropolitan area, and submitted the
following report, part of which is quoted here.

Source: U.S. Congress, Joint Committee on Washington Metropolitan
Problems, Growth and Expansion of the District of Columbia and its
Metropolitan Area; Progress Report, Washington, 1958.

DEFINITION OF THE WASHINGTON METROPOLITAN REGION

The committee's studies will be conducted within the general
framework of the Washington metropolitan region. The definition of
this region which the committee will use in its studies includes the
Maryland counties of Prince Georges and Montgomery, the Virginia
counties of Arlington and Fairfax, and the District of Columbia. It
also includes numerous independent cities lying within these limits.
The area so bounded conforms to the standard metropolitan area as
defined by the Bureau of the Census. Thus, the boundary coincides
with major statistical and research activities, an obvious advantage
to the committee in its study (see exhibit No. 1).
The definition of the region reflects the criteria for defining
metropolitan problems to be considered by the committee in the first
part of its work program. These criteria are the areawide scope of
the problem; the desirability and economy of handling it on a unified
basis rather than piecemeal by jurisdictions; its interest to the area
as a whole as it relates to growth and well-being of the metropolitan
region; and its uniqueness in the sense that only a metropolitan area
organization would be able to deal with the problem.
Beyond this regional boundary, the committee will have to consider in some of its studies, the entire drainage basin of the Potomac
River (see exhibit No. 2), and the position of the Washington metropolitan region as part of the continuous urban belt reaching north along
the Atlantic coast (see exhibit No. 3). The Potomac drainage basin
will contain factors affecting the metropolitan water supply. To the
northeast, the rapidly growing and expanding Baltimore metropolitan
area meets the Washington metropolitan area at the Patuxent River,
and in certain functions overlaps with it. Coordination with the studies
of the Baltimore Regional Planning Council has been effected by the
committee's staff.
The committee will also have to consider the area under the
jurisdiction of the National Capital Regional Planning Council (as
defined in the National Capital Planning Act of 1952, Public Law 592,
82d Cong., 2d sess.) which embraces two additional Virginia counties,

Loudoun and Prince William. While this area has a distinct value in studying the metropolitan region, particularly looking to its future, the smaller regional boundaries chosen conform more exactly to the present metropolitan population and the incidence of metropolitan problems.

The Interstate Commerce Commission used a definition of the Washington commercial zone that is more restrictive than the Census standard metropolitan area.

The Joint Commission To Study Passenger Carrier Facilities in the Washington metropolitan area has created a regional definition of the mass transportation service area as follows: In Maryland the following election districts in Montgomery County (Rockville, Colesville, Bethesda, Potomac, Wheaton, Olney, and Gaithersburg) and Prince Vansvill, Lanham, Kent, Seat Pleasant, Spauldings, Surratts, and Oxon Hill); and in Virginia the following magistral districts in Fairfax County (Falls Church, Mason, Mount Vernon, and Providence) and the whole of Arlington County and the independent cities of Alexandria and Falls Church. An additional area in Maryland, embracing the Montgomery election district of Clarksburg, and the Prince Georges election districts of Laurel and Bowie, allows the joint commission transit service area to embrace that part of the metropolitan area served only by bus.

Numerous other service districts have been defined, illustrating the close relationship between the central city and its suburban neighbors.

GROWTH OF POPULATION OF THE WASHINGTON METROPOLITAN REGION

The present population of the Washington metropolitan region is slightly more than 2,000,000.

The census of 1950 found the following population by major subdivisions:

District of Columbia	802,178
Montgomery County, Md	164,401
Prince Georges County, Md	194,182
Arlington County, Va	135,449
Fairfax County, Va	98,557
Alexandria, Va	61,787
Falls Church, Va	7,535

The past growth of population has been extremely rapid. Between 1940 and 1950, the metropolitan area population increased by 51.3 percent. Among standard metropolitan areas whose total population exceeding 1 million, the Washington area was the second fastest growing.

As is the case with most metropolitan areas, the rate of growth of the surrounding areas is considerably more rapid than the older, built-up central city.

Estimates of future population growth have been prepared. The most recent official estimate, prepared by the National Capital Regional

Planning Council in the course of its mass transportation study, yielded two figures. These refer to the Council's regional area, including Loudoun and Prince William Counties. On the assumption of no further industrialization than at present, an estimate of about 2.3 million by 1965 and 2.8 million by 1980 was reached. On the assumption full industrialization was achieved by 1980, the Council's estimated population was 2.9 million by 1965 and 4.8 million by 1980.

Careful population estimates have also been made by the Washington Board of Trade Economic Development Committee. (These estimates refer to the standard metropolitan area.) These assumed a population of 3.5 million by 1980 and of 4.8 million for the year 2000.

Further details are not necessary to establish the fact that the Washington metropolitan area is one of the Nation's most rapidly growing urban concentrations. In terms of population rank, the region moved from 16th largest in 1930 to 11th in 1950. Today it is considered the ninth largest metropolitan area, and by 1980 is expected to be the seventh largest.

EXPANSION OF THE WASHINGTON METROPOLITAN REGION

The expansion of the Washington metropolitan area is graphically illustrated by the accompanying series of maps (see exhibit No. 4). While an exceptionally rapid period of growth occurred in the period 1927 to 1947, reflecting the expansion of the city during the 1930's and the war years, settlement tended to be relatively contiguous, following the major transportation lines. The postwar years have seen a rapid acceleration in the area's growth and expansion but, of greater significance, a new pattern of settlement appeared. As may be noted in the outlying urban development shown in the 1955 map, this was far more scattered, amorphous, sprawling. It reflected the almost universal suburban use of the automobile, the rise of subregional shopping and service centers, new decentralized locations of employment, and a new pattern of home building. Providing the public services needed by this new suburban population in its highly decentralized location is a major new problem of local governments. Knitting these new areas into the economic and political structure of the metropolitan region as a whole, and to its central area in particular, constitutes a major problem if metropolitan unification is to be achieved.

The extremely decentralized and diffused pattern of suburban settlement that has appeared in recent years is a formidable background to the solution of metropolitan problems of water, sewage disposal, transportation and other services. . . .

THE TWENTY-THIRD AMENDMENT -- 1961

The passage of the Twenty-third Amendment to the Constitution on June 16, 1960, and its subsequent ratification on April 3, 1961, struck away the limitation on voting rights derived from residence in the District of Columbia. This amendment follows.

Source: Twenty-Third Amendment, Constitution of the United States.

Article XXIII

Section 1. The District constituting the seat of Government of the United States shall appoint in such manner as the Congress may direct:

A number of electors of President and Vice-President equal to the whole number of Senators and Representatives in Congress to which the District would be entitled if it were a State, but in no event more than the least populous State; they shall be in addition to those appointed by the States, but they shall be considered, for the purposes of the election of President and Vice-President, to be electors appointed by a State; and they shall meet in the District and perform such duties as provided by the twelfth article of amendment.

Section 2. The Congress shall have power to enforce this article by appropriate legislation.

THE DISTRICT REORGANIZATION PLAN -- 1967

The Reorganization Plan for the District of Columbia, sponsored by President Lyndon Johnson, became fully effective on
November 3, 1967. The district commissioners were replaced
by a presidentially appointed mayor, deputy mayor, and a nine
man bi-partisan council. This was the city's new charter.

Source: District of Columbia Code, 1967 Edition, Cumulative Supplement IV, Washington, D.C. 1971.

GOVERNMENT OF THE DISTRICT OF COLUMBIA

PART I. GENERAL PROVISIONS

Section 101. Definitions. (a) As used in this reorganization plan,
plan, the term "the Corporation" means the body-corporate for municipal purposes created a government by the name of the "District
of Columbia."

(b) References in this reorganization plan to any provision of the
District of Columbia Code are references to the provisions of statutory
law codified under that provision and include the said provision as
amended, modified, or supplemented prior to the effective date of this
reorganization plan (including modifications made by Reorganization
Plan No. 5 of 1952 (66 Stat. 824)).

Sec. 102. Reorganization. The Corporation is hereby reorganized
as provided in the following Parts of this reorganization plan.

PART II. DISTRICT OF COLUMBIA COUNCIL

Sec. 201. Establishment of the Council. (a) There is hereby established in the Corporation a Council which shall be known as the "District of Columbia Council" (hereinafter referred to as the Council).

(b) The Council shall be composed of a Chairman of the Council,
a Vice Chairman of the Council, and seven other members, all of whom
shall be appointed by the President of the United States, by and with the
advice and consent of the Senate. At the time of his appointment each
member of the Council shall be a citizen of the United States, shall
have been an actual resident of the District of Columbia for three years
next preceding his appointment, and shall during that period have
claimed residence nowhere else. The Council shall be nonpartisan
and no more than six of its members shall be adherents of any one
political party. Appointments to the Council shall be made with a view
toward achieving a Council membership which will be broadly representative of the District of Columbia community.

(c) One or more of the nine Council members hereinabove provided for may be appointed from among (1) retired civilian employees

of the Government, (2) retired personnel of the armed services of the United States, and (3) retired personnel of the Corporation. Any person so appointed shall be eligible to receive the compensation provided for in section 204 hereof and appointment hereunder shall not affect his right to receive annuity, pension, or retired pay to which he is otherwise entitled.

(d) Three of the appointments first made under this section shall be for terms expiring February 1, 1968, three shall be for terms expiring February 1, 1969, and three shall be for terms expiring February 1, 1970; and thereafter appointments shall be made for terms of three years. Any appointment made to fill a vacancy shall be made only for the unexpired balance of the term. Any member of the Council may continue to serve as such member after the expiration of his term of office until his successor is appointed and qualifies. Any member of the Council may be removed by the President of the United States for neglect of duty or malfeasance in office or when the member has been found guilty of a felony or conduct involving moral turpitude.

(e) Each member of the Council before entering upon the discharge of his duties as such member shall take an oath or affirmation to support the Constitution of the United States and to faithfully discharge the duties imposed upon him as such member.

(f) Five members of the Council shall constitute a quorum for the transaction of business of the Council, except that four members shall constitute a quorum whenever two or more Council memberships are vacant.

Sec. 202. Acting Chairman. During the absence or disability of the Chairman of the Council, or whenever there be no Chairman, the Vice Chairman shall act as Chairman of the Council.

Sec. 203. Secretary of the Council. (a) There is hereby established the office of the Secretary of the Council. The Secretary shall be appointed by the Council from time to time.

(b) The Secretary shall perform such duties, and shall provide such services for the Council and its members, as the Council may prescribe. Personnel appointed to assist the Secretary in carrying out his responsibilities under this section shall be appointed by the Secretary subject to the approval of the Council.

Sec. 204. Compensation. The Chairman of the Council shall receive compensation at the rate of $10,000 per annum, the Vice Chairman shall receive compensation at the rate of $9,000 per annum, and each other member of the Council shall receive compensation at the rate of $7,500 per annum. The Secretary of the Council shall receive compensation determined in accordance with the classification laws as amended from time to time.

Sec. 205. Performance of functions of the Council. (a) The Council is hereby authorized to make from time to time such provisions as it deems appropriate to authorize the performance of any of its functions by the Commissioner of the District of Columbia (herinafter provided for).

(b) The Council is hereby authorized to make from time to time, subject to the concurrence of the Commissioner of the District of

Columbia, such provisions as it deems appropriate to authorize the performance of any of its functions by any officer, agency, or employee of the Corporation except the courts thereof.

(c) All functions provided for in regulations continued in force without action by the Council) which are to be carried out by any officer, employee, or agency, who or which is in other respects under the jurisdiction of the Commissioner of the District of Columbia shall be carried out by such officer, employee, or agency under the direction and control of the Commissioner.

PART III. COMMISSIONER OF THE DISTRICT OF COLUMBIA

Sec. 301. Establishment of office of Commissioner. (a) There is hereby established in the Corporation an office with the title of "Commissioner of the District of Columbia." The officer who holds that office is hereinafter referred to as the Commissioner.

(b) The Commissioner shall be appointed by the President of the United States, by and with the advice and consent of the Senate. The Commissioner shall at the time of his appointment be a citizen of the United States. Before entering upon the discharge of his duties the Commissioner shall take an oath or affirmation to support the Constitution of the United States and faithfully discharge the duties imposed upon him as Commissioner. The Commissioner shall receive compensation at the rate now or hereafter prescribed by law for offices and positions of Level III of the Executive Schedule Pay Rates (5 U.S.C. 5314). Whenever both a Commissioner and an Assistant to the Commissioner appointed under section 312 hereof are in office at least one of them shall have been an actual resident of the District of Columbia for three years next preceding his appointment and have during that period claimed residence nowhere else. Both the Commissioner and the Assistant to the Commissioner shall reside in the District of Columbia during the time each holds office.

(c) The first appointment of a Commissioner hereunder shall be for a term expiring on February 1, 1969, and thereafter each appointment shall be made for a term of four years. Any appointment made to fill a vacancy in the office shall be made only for the unexpired balance of the term. A Commissioner may continue to serve as such after the expiration of his term of office until his successor is appointed and qualifies. The Commissioner is subject to removal by the President of the United States.

(d) The President may from time to time (1) designate officials of the Corporation (including the Chairman, the Vice Chairman, and the other members of the Council provided for in Part II of this reorganization plan if the President so elects) to act as Commissioner during the absence or disability of the Commissioner or in the event of a vacancy in the office of Commissioner, and (2) prescribe the order of succession in which the officials so designate shall so act.

Sec. 302. Assistant to the Commissioner. There is hereby established in the Corporation a new office which shall have the title "Assistant to the Commissioner of the District of Columbia." . . . .

THE WASHINGTON RIOTS -- 1968

The murder of Martin Luther King Jr. in Memphis evoked a reaction of intense anger in many American cities among the black community. In Washington three days of violent rioting took place culminating in President Lyndon B. Johnson's calling out the Regular Army and National Guard to quell the disturbances. The following selections are description of the rioting and President Johnson's Proclamation and Executive Order on the disorders in the Nation's Capital.

Source: New York Times, April 5, 1968; Government Printing Office, The Public Papers of the Presidents: Lyndon B. Johnson, 1963-1969, 9 vols., Washington, D.C., 1966-1969.

President Johnson ordered 4,000 regular Army and National Guard troops into the nation's capital tonight to try to end riotous looting, burglarizing and burning by roving bands of Negro youths. The arson and looting began yesterday after the murder of the Rev. Dr. Martin Luther King Jr. in Memphis.

The White House announced at 5 P.M. that because the President had determined that, "a condition of domestic violence and disorder" existed, he had issued a proclamation and an Executive order mobilizing combat-equipped troops in Washington. Some of the troops were sent to guard the Capitol and the White House.

Reinforcements numbering 2,500 riot-trained soldiers -- a brigade of the 82d Airborne Division from Ft. Bragg, N.C. -- were airlifted to nearby Andrews Air Force Base, to be held in reserve this weekend.

Guard Called In Other Cities

The National Guard also was called out in a half-dozen other cities in an effort to stem disorders or guard against them -- Chicago, Detroit, Boston, Jackson, Miss., Raleigh, N. C., and Tallahassee, Fla.

The death toll from the violence stemming from Dr. King's assassination stood at a total of 14 tonight. Besides five deaths in Washington, they included seven in Chicago, one in Detroit and one in Tallahassee.

Mayor Walter E. Washington, who is a Negro, declared a 13-hour curfew, from 5:30 P.M. to 6:30 A.M. The Mayor's emergency order halted the sale of liquor and forbade the sale, transportation or possession of firearms, explosives or flammable liquids.

At midnight, the police reported five dead; all but one of them Negroes, in 28 hours of disorders in this city of about 800,000, 63 per cent of them Negroes. Four Negroes were killed today, including two suspected looters, one of them 14 years old who were shot to death by policemen in separate isolated encounters across the Anacostia River, far from the areas of general disorders. The two other Negro deaths today were described as apparently the result of accidents.

The white man, George Fletcher, 28, of surburban Woodbridge, Va., died this morning from injuries he received when a gang of Negro youths attacked him and three white companions in a Washington filling station at 2 A.M.

More than 350 persons were treated at hospitals including seven policemen and six firemen. More than 800 persons were arrested.

The police said reports of fires and lootings were diminishing apparently in part due to a sudden drop in the temperature. After a sultry day, the night air was a brisk 40 degrees.

The violence in Washington affected four areas of the city. For hours this afternoon and early evening, disorderly youths roamed most of the downtown shopping district, between 15th and Seventh Streets and F and H Streets N.W.

The three other areas were all Negro sections. There was no precise count of the number of fires or looted stores, but they ran well into the hundreds.

George Christian, the White House press secretary said the President had acted on the recommendation of Mayor Washington, the Mayor's public safety director, Patrick V. Murphy, and the police chief, John B. Layton.

The 2,800-man District of Columbia police force, after a night of looting and arson set off yesterday by the assassination, lacked the manpower to respond to mounting calls to detain looters and protect motorists and firemen.

The looting and fires continued tonight. The police dispersed crowds as they gathered but made little or no effort to stop scattered-looting by individuals and groups of two and three.

The city was abandoned tonight. Buses stopped running at dusk after a midafternoon rush of Government employes to flee the city. The Government workers and other civilians were advised by the police and Federal authorities to go home at about 2:30 P.M., a decision that caused a massive traffic jam and aided the looters. Police and fire vehicles were caught in the jam.

Tourists Affected

Also caught up in the unexpected disturbances were Washington's spring crush of thousands of tourists. Events scheduled for today and the weekend in connection with the Washington Cherry Blossom Festival-- a major money-making attraction in this city where tourism is the biggest industry -- were canceled.

The opening game of the American baseball season, the American League debut between the Washington Senators and the Minnesota Twins at D. C. Stadium, was postponed from Monday to Tuesday as a gesture of respect to Dr. King.

Both the outbreak of trouble last night and today's renewal of arson and looting followed angry public outbursts on Dr. King's death by Stokely Carmichael, the militant former chairman of the Student Nonviolent Coordinating Committee. He has been active as a committee field representative in Washington since his return from an around-the-world trip last January.

The looting last night followed a protest march led by Carmichael down 14th Street N.W., the center of a principal Negro commercial and shopping area. He demanded that businesses close for the night as a gesture of mourning for Dr. King. Then he urged Negroes to "go home and get your guns."

A Breathing Spell

By dawn 14th Street was a shambles of shattered glass and scattered merchandise. But sunlight brought a breathing spell. Sanitation workers began shoveling up the shards of glass.

At 10 A.M. Carmichael called a news conference at the 14th Street headquarters of the New School for Afro-American Thought. Before television cameras he declared that "white America has declared war on black America" with the murder of Dr. King.

There is "no alternative to retribution," he said.

"Black people have to survive, and the only way they will survive is by getting guns," he said.

Less than an hour after the 30-minute news conference ended, Carmichael was in the street with a following of 50 Negroes. Both newsmen and the police lost track of him as the day progressed.

The police either could not or would not interfere with the looting, and much of it was done brazenly, under the gaze of outnumbered police officers. Loot was hauled away in automobiles and trucks. During most of the afternoon the police dealt only with large groups of looters and a seemingly endless series of fires.

In the downtown shopping area of large department and specialty stores, the windows of such stores as Hecht's and Woodward and Lothrop's were smashed and looted. There were fires at both stores. The police appeared to concentrate their protective maneuvers along F Street, giving the other areas less priority.

In the second area hit, along Seventh Street N.W. from K to P. Streets, looting and fires -- the major fires of the day were concentrated there -- gradually drained off the scattered police manpower.

In a third area, looters and firebombers struck along 14th Street from downtown F Street as far north as Park Road N.W., nearly halfway to the Maryland line at Silver Spring.

Another less well defined area of looting and arson was across the Anacostia River, in heavily Negro Southeast Washington. Two of today's deaths occurred there.

North and West of the city, the two contiguous suburban jurisdictions in Maryland, Montgomery and Prince Georges Counties, both declared local emergencies during the day, invoking most of the special powers, with the exception of a curfew, authorized in the city. More than 50 pieces of fire equipment from volunteer companies in suburban counties were rushed into the city during the afternoon to aid the overtaxed district fire department. . . .

PRESIDENTIAL PROCLAMATION

By the President of the United States of America

A Proclamation

WHEREAS I have been informed that conditions of domestic violence and disorder exist in the District of Columbia and threaten the
Washington metropolitan area, endangering life and property and ob-
structing execution of the laws, and the local police forces are unable
to bring about the prompt cessation of such acts of violence and restoration of law and order; and

WHEREAS I have been requested to use such units of the National
Guard and of the armed forces of the United States as may be necessary
for these purposes; and

WHEREAS in such circumstances it is also my duty as Chief
Executive to take care that the property, personnel and functions of the
Federal Government, of embassies of foreign governments, and of
international organizations in the Washington metropolitan area are
protected against violence or other interference:

NOW, THEREFORE, I, Lyndon B. Johnson, President of the United
States of America, by virtue of the authority vested in me by the Constitution and laws of the United States, do command all persons engaged
in such acts of violence to desist therefrom and to disperse and retire
peaceably forthwith.

IN WITNESS THEREOF, I have hereunto set my hand this fifth
day of April, in the year of Our Lord nineteen hundred and sixty-eight,
and of the independence of the United States of America the one hundred
and ninety-second.

Lyndon B. Johnson.

Executive Order

Providing for the restoration of law and order in the Washington
metropolitan area.

WHEREAS, I have today issued Proclamation 3840, calling upon
persons engaged in acts of violence and disorder in the Washington
metropolitan area to cease and desist therefrom and to disperse and
retire peaceably forthwith and,

WHEREAS, the conditions of domestic violence and disorder
described therein continue, and the persons engaging in such acts of
violence have not dispersed:

NOW, THEREFORE, by virtue of the authority vested in me as President of the United States and Commander in Chief of the armed forces
under the Constitution and laws of the United States, including Chapter
15 of Title 10 of the United States Code and Section 301 of Title 3 of the
United States Code, and by virtue of the authority vested in me as

Commander in Chief of the militia of the District of Columbia by the Act of March 1, 1889, as amended (D.C. Code, Title 39), is hereby ordered as follows:

Section 1. The Secretary of Defense is authorized and directed to take all appropriate steps to disperse all persons engaged in the acts of violence described in the Proclamation, to restore law and order, and to see that the property, personnel and functions of the Federal Government, of embassies of foreign governments, and of international organizations in the Washington metropolitan area are protected against violence or other interference.

Section 2. In carrying out the provisions of Section 1, the Secretary of Defense is authorized to use such of the armed forces of the United States as he may deem necessary.

Section 3. (A) The Secretary of Defense is hereby authorized and directed to call into the active military service of the United States, as he may deem appropriate to carry out the purposes of this order, units or members of the Army National Guard and of the Air National Guard to serve in the active military service of the United States for an indefinite period and until relieved by appropriate orders. Units or members may be relieved subject to recall at the discretion of the Secretary of Defense. In carrying out the provisions of Section 1, the Secretary of Defense is authorized to use units and members called or recalled into active military service of the United States pursuant to this section.

(B) In addition, in carrying out the provisions of Sections 1, the Secretary of Defense is authorized to exercise any of the powers vested in me by law as Commander in Chief of the militia of the District of Columbia, during such times as any units or members of the Army National Guard or Air National Guard of the district shall not have been called into the active military service of the United States.

Section 4. The Secretary of Defense is authorized to delegate to one or more of the secretaries of the military departments any of the authority conferred upon him by this order.

LYNDON B. JOHNSON,
THE WHITE HOUSE
April 5, 1968

SELF-GOVERNMENT FOR WASHINGTON -- 1969

President Richard M. Nixon proposed a series of steps to improve the District's government, including a self-government
charter and voting representation in the House and Senate. A
portion of his speech to Congress on this matter follows.

Source: Public Papers of the Presidents of the United States, Richard
M. Nixon, vol. I, Washington, 1971.

To the Congress of the United States:

Carved out of swampland at our country's birth, the Nation's
Capital city now sets a new test of national purpose. This was a city
that men dared to plan -- and build by plan -- laying out avenues and
monuments and housing in accordance with a common rational scheme.
Now we are challenged once again to shape our environment: to renew
our city by rational foresight and planning, rather than leaving it to
grow swamp-like without design.
At issue is whether the city will be enabled to take hold of its
future: whether its institutions will be reformed so that its government can truly represent it citizens and act upon their needs.
Good government, in the case of a city, must be local government.
The Federal Government has a special responsibility for the District
of Columbia. But it also bears toward the District the same responsibility it bears toward all other cities: to help local government work
better, and to attempt to supplement local resources for programs that
city officials judge most urgent.
My aim is to increase the responsibility and efficiency of the
District of Columbia's new government, which has performed so ably
during its first perilous years. Early in this Administration, we recommended proposals that would increase the effectiveness of local law
enforcement and provide the resources needed by local officials to
begin revitalizing the areas damaged during the civil disturbance. Those
proposals, however, cover only a part of the program which will be
essential for the District Government to respond to the wishes of its
people.
I now present the second part of this program, worked out in
close consultation with the District Government, and based upon the
needs articulated by the Mayor and the City Council.
This program will provide:
-- An orderly mechanism for achieving self-government in the
   District of Columbia.
-- Representation in Congress.
-- Added municipal authority for the City Council and the Mayor.
-- Additional top management positions to bring new talents and
   leadership into the District Government.

-- A secure and equitable source of Federal funds for the District's budget.

-- An expanded rapid rail transit system, linking the diverse segments of our Capital's metropolitan region.

The Federal Government bears a major responsibility for the welfare of our Capital's citizens in general. It owns much of the District's land and employs many of its citizens. It depends on the services of local government. The condition of our Capital city is a sign of the condition of our nation -- and is certainly taken as such by visitors, from all the states of the Union, and from around the globe.

However, this Federal responsibility does not require Federal rule. Besides the official Washington of monuments and offices, there is the Washington of 850,000 citizens with all the hopes and expectations of the people of any major city, striving and sacrificing for a better life -- the eighth largest among the cities of our country.

Self-Government

Full citizenship through local self-government must be given to the people of this city: The District Government cannot be truly responsible until it is made responsible to those who live under its rule. The District's citizens should not be expected to pay taxes for a government which they have no part in choosing -- or to bear the full burdens of citizenship without the full rights of citizenship.

I therefore ask Congress to create a Commission on Self-Government for the District of Columbia, to be charged with submitting to Congress and the President a proposal for establishing meaningful self-government in the District.

In order for any government to be accountable to the people, responsibilities must be clearly pinpointed, and officials must have the powers they need to carry out their responsibilities. The Commission would recommend how best to augment and allocate the legislative and executive authorities with respect to governing the city.

The members of this Commission would be partly appointed by the President, partly designated by the Congress, and partly chosen in a city-wide election by the citizens of the District. They would be given an adequate but strictly defined time period to formulate their plan. I would hope that the Commission would be established promptly, so that its report could be submitted to Congress and the President in time for the 1970 legislative session. With adequate funding, they would be able to draw on the wisdom of consultants throughout the country -- men who know firsthand the art of the possible, as well as those who study government -- in addition to their own staff.

The Commission members must give thorough consideration to the many alternative plans for self-government which have been presented over the years. But they must also make use of new knowledge we have gained about the problems of existing local government around the country -- in finance, management, urban development, citizen participation and many other areas. They must seek the sentiment of the District's citizens from the earliest stages of their work.

There also is a Federal interest that must be respected. The
normal functions of the Federal agencies must be guaranteed and their
vital operations protected. There must be continued Federal jurisdiction
over public buildings and monuments and assurance of well-being for
the men and women who work in them or come to visit. The rights of
the national government must be protected, at the same time as the
rights of the city's residents are secured. There must be respect for
the responsibilities with regard to the District which the Constitution
places in the Congress.

To establish a new government in so diverse and active a city
as the District is certainly no easy task. There are dangers in setting
up new governments, as well as opportunities. Congress has been rightly
concerned that the plan for self-government must insure responsible
elections, effective executive leadership, protection of individual liberty
and safeguards for District of Columbia employees. Self-government must
be extended in a timely and orderly manner.

It is especially important that the Commission go beyond the issue
of self-government as such, and concern itself with the effective func-
tioning of government in the District of Columbia. Under the existing
government structure the City Council finds itself without the power
to deal with many crucial problems because of the conflicting and
divided authorities that now reside in independent agencies.

But there is no cause for delay: Self-government has remained
an unfulfilled promise for far too long. It has been energetically supported
by the past four Presidents -- Harry S. Truman, Dwight D. Eisenhower,
John F. Kennedy, and Lyndon B. Johnson. The Senate approved measures
to provide it during the 81st, 82nd, 84th, and 86th Congresses. We owe
the present lack of local elections to the Reconstruction period, when
Congress rescued the District from bankruptcy but suspended the voting
franchise. Congress established the Commission form of government
in 1874 as a temporary "receivership," but the Commissioners' government persisted for over 90 years -- and today, even after reorganization in 1967, the District remains under Federal control.

The history of failure for self-government proposals shows the
need for a new plan strong enough to stand up against the old questions
or criticisms. Myriad different plans have been offered -- and will be
offered again this year. But each will have its own doubters as well as
its supporters. A Commission must examine all of them, combining old
and new ideas in a proposal that will at last win the broad-based respect
necessary for final acceptance, and that will carry the authority of a
disinterested group of men whose vocation is government -- jurists,
political leaders and scholars, as well as other citizens, investing the
wisdom of their life's work in a truly new government. . . .

BIBLIOGRAPHY

The bibliography section of this book, represents a varied selection of some of the best known and most useful primary and secondary works on the City of Washington and the District of Columbia. Because of the fact that Washington was and still is the nation's capital, the official records are not only abundant but also extremely informative. The sheer mass of both published and unpublished primary materials, if compiled in lists, would encompass a total of printed pages equal to or greater than this entire volume. For this reason, the author has confined his bibliographical choices to certain selected works; and, even with these, as a result of space limitations, he has been forced to be highly discriminating in his choice of pertinant materials. Nevertheless, the titles chosen for this bibliography provide the reader with an excellent starting point to begin or further his research into this facinating and extremely complex city.

All of the primary materials concerned with the City of Washington and the District of Columbia can be found in the National Archives, the Library of Congress, and the Washingtoniana Room of the District Public Library. In addition, most local libraries contain fairly good collections of secondary materials dealing with the city.

PRIMARY SOURCES

Annual Reports of the Alley Dwelling Authority for the District of
    Columbia. Washington, 1935.

Annual Reports of the Board of Charities of the District of Columbia.
    Washington, 1901-1925.

Annual Reports of Children's Guardians of the District of Columbia.
    1893-1925. Washington, 1925.

Annual Reports of the Board of Education of the District of Columbia.
    Washington, 1901-1950.

Annual Reports of the Board of Public Welfare of the District of Columbia.
    Washington, 1926-1932, 1934-1960.

Annual Reports of the Commissioners of the District of Columbia, 1879-
    1935, continued as Government of the District of Columbia. Wash-
    ington, 1936-1960.

Annual Reports of the Fine Arts Commission. Washington, 1911-1932.

Annual Reports of the National Capital Park and Planning Commission.
    Washington, 1927-1932.

Annual Reports of the Proceedings of the U.S. National Museum. Washing-
    ton. 1911, 1916.

Annual Reports of the Smithsonian Institution. Washington, 1847-1970.

Code of Laws of the District of Columbia. 1929, 1951.

Congressional Globe. 46 vols. Washington, 1834-1873.

Congressional Record. Washington, 1873-1970.

Corporation of the City of Washington. Acts. 11 vols. Washington, 1805-
    1816, Continued as Laws of the Corporation of the City of Washing-
    ton. 45 vols. Washington, 1817-1862.

Journals of the Council of the City of Washington. Washington, 1864-1871.

Journals of the Council of the District of Columbia. 5 vols. Washington,
    1872-1874.

Journals of the House of Delegates of the District of Columbia. 5 vols.

Washington, 1871-1873.

National Capital Park and Planning Commission. Washington, Past and Future. Washington, 1950.

National Gallery of Art. Bulletins. Washington, 1941-1970.

Reports of the President's Homes Commission. Washington, 1908.

Rothwell, Andrew. Laws of the Corporation of the City of Washington. Washington, 1833.

Sheahan, James. Corporation Laws of the City of Washington. Washington, 1853.

Strayer, George D. Report of a Survey of the Public Schools of the District of Columbia, conducted under the auspices of the chairmen of the sub-committees on District of Columbia appropriations of the respective committees of the Senate and House. Washington, 1949.

Washington Board of Health. Reports. Washington, 1856-1910.

Washington Board of Trade. Annual Reports. Washington, 1890-1929, 1936-1940.

Webb, William B. The Laws of the Corporation of the City of Washington. Washington, 1868.

SECONDARY SOURCES

Abell, George, and Gordon, Evelyn. Let Them Eat Caviar. New York, 1936. Amusing story of Washington society.

American Institute of Architects. Of Plans and People. Washington, 1949. Interesting study of planning and engineering in the nation's capital.

_____. A Committee of the Washington Metropolitan Chapter. Washington Architecture, 1791-1957. Washington, 1957.

(Anon). The Mirrors of Washington. London, 1921.

(Anon). Washington Merry go-round. New York, 1931. Lively, journalistic study of anecdotal material.

At Lee, Samuel Yorke. History of the Public Schools of Washington City, D.C., from August, 1805 to August, 1875. Washington, 1876.

Barton, Elmer E. Historical and Commercial Sketches of Washington and Envoirons, Our Capital City, The Paris of America. Washington, 1884.

Belden, Thomas A., and Marva R. So Fell the Angels. Boston, 1956.

Bicknell, Grace V. The Inhabited Alleys of Washington, D.C. Washington, 1912. Old, but useful study of one of Washington's most serious historic problems.

Brooks, Noah. Washington in Lincoln's Time. New York. 1895. Although old, contains excellent description of the city during the 1860's.

Brown, Glenn. Memories: A Winning Crusade to Revive George Washington's Vision of a Capital City. Washington, 1931.

_____. History of the United States Capital. 2 vols. Washington, 1900-1903. An old, but still useful work as far as it goes.

Browne, Henry J. Assessment and Taxation in the District of Columbia and the Fiscal Relation to the Federal Government. Washington, 1915. Detailed work on the problem of financing the city government and programs.

Brownlow, Louis. A Passion for Politics. Chicago, 1955. Very interesting autobiographical study by one of the District Commissioners.

Bryan, Wilhelmus B. A History of the National Capital. 2 vols. New York, 1914-1916. Although dated, an excellent, detailed work on the development of the city.

Bulkley, Barry. Washington, Old and New. Washington, 1914.

Cahnmerer, Paul H. The Life of Pierre Charles L'Enfant. Washington, 1950. Solid, scholarly biography of the great architect.

Chapin, Elizabeth M. American Court Gossip, or Life at the Nation's Capital. Marshalltown, Iowa. 1887.

Church of God, A Picturial Review. Washington, 1944. A revealing pictorial essay of Elder Michaux and the church he founded in the city.

Clark, Allen C. Greenleaf and Law in the Federal City. Washington, 1901.

Clephone, Walter C. Public and Private Hospitals in the District of Columbia. Washington, 1912.

Coulson, Thomas. Joseph Henry, His Life and Work. Princeton, 1950. Excellent biography of the first secretary of the Smithsonian Institution.

Crane, Katherine E. Blair House, Past and Present. Washington, 1945. Fascinating study of one of Washington's most historic houses.

_____. Mr. Carr of State. New York, 1960.

Crew, H.W. Centennial History of the City of Washington. Washington, 1901. Interesting anecdotal history of the capital.

Dahlgren, Madeleine V. Etiquette of Social Life in Washington. 5th ed. Philadelphia, 1881. Dated etiquette book written by the self-styled leader of Washington society.

Darrah, William C. Powell of the Colorado. Princeton, 1951. Very good biography of one of Washington's leading citizens of the nineteenth century.

D.C. Village. Fifty Years at Blue Plains, 1906-1956. Washington, 1957.

District of Columbia Engineers' Office. Washington Bridges, 1945.

Douglass, Frederick. Life and Times of Frederick Douglass. New York, 1893. Moving autobiography of the great Negro leader, and the role he played in Washington's history.

Dupree, A. Hunter. Science in the Federal Government, A History of Policies and Activities to 1940. Cambridge, 1957. Most of the major scientific trends and accomplishments in the capital are discussed and evaluated.

Fairman, Charles E. Art and Artists of the Capitol of the United States of America. Washington, 1927. Solid work with excellent illustrations and reproductions.

Federal Writers' Project. Washington: City and Capital. Washington, 1937. One of the best works produced under W.P.A. auspices.

Fleming, Walter L. The Freedman's Savings Bank: A Chapter in the Economic History of the Negro Race. Chapel Hill, 1937. Scholarly study of the great Negro banking institution in Washington.

Goode, George B. The Genesis of the United States National Museum in Report of the U.S. National Museum. 1891.

Gray, Edgar M. The Washington Race Riot, Its Cause and Effect. New York, 1919. Excellent evaluation of the bitter race riot in the nation's capital.

Green, Constance M. The Secret City: A History of Race Relations in the Nation's Capital. Princeton, 1957. Brilliant, detailed volume on one of Washington's most complex problems.

_____. Washington: Village and Capital. 1800-1878. Princeton, 1962. Probably the best work on the history of the city. Contains an excellent bibliography.

_____. Washington: Capital City, 1879-1950. Princeton, 1963. Second
volume of this excellent study.

Grier, Eunice. Understanding Washington's Population. Washington,
1961. Very good work on the city's population trends.

Hagedorn, Herman. Robert Brookings: A Biography. New York, 1936.
Solid biography on the industrialist-philanthropist.

Hart, Hastings H. Child Welfare in the District of Columbia. New York,
1924.

Hayes, Lawrence J.W. The Negro Federal Government Worker: A study
of his Classification Status in the District of Columbia, 1883-1938.
Washington, 1941.

Hibben, Henry B. Navy Yard, Washington. History from Organization,
1799 to present date. Washington, 1890.

History of the League of Women Voters of the District of Columbia.
Washington, 1960.

Hungerford, Edward. The Story of the Baltimore and Ohio Railroad,
1827-1927. 2 vols. New York, 1928. Very good history of the famous
railroad, and the part it played in the growth of Washington.

Hurd, Charles. Washington Cavalcade. New York, 1948.

Hyman, Harold M. Era of the Oath, Northern Loyalty Texts During the
Civil War and Reconstruction. Philadelphia, 1954. Solid study
covering Washington's dilemma during this critical period.

Ingle, Edward. The Negro in the District of Columbia, in Johns Hopkins
University Studies in History and Political Science. 11th Series.
Nos. III and IV.

Jackson, Richard P. The Chronicles of Georgetown, D.C. from 1751
to 1878. Washington, 1878.

Jacobsen, H.N. A Guide to the Architecture of Washington. Washington,
1965.

Johnson, Lorenzo D. The Churches and Pastors of Washington, D.C.
New York, 1857.

Jones, William H. Recreation and Amusement Among Negroes in
Washington, D.C.; A Sociological Analysis of the Negro in an
Urban Environment. Washington, 1927.

_____ . The Housing of Negroes in Washington, D.C.: A Study in Human Ecology. Washington, 1929. Although dated, contains some excellent information.

Keim, De Benneville Randolph. Society in Washington, Its Noted Men, Accomplished Women, Established Customs, and Notable Events. Harrisburg, Pa., 1887.

Kite, Elizabeth S. L'Enfant and Washington, 1791-1792. Baltimore, 1929. Detailed study of the great architect and his role in the planning of the national capital.

Knox, Ellis, O. Democracy and the District of Columbia Schools: A Study of Recently Integrated Schools. Washington, 1957.

Kober, George M. The History and Development of the Housing Movement in the City of Washington, D.C. Washington, 1907.

Leech, Margaret. Reveille in Washington. New York, 1941. Brilliant prize winning book concerning the city during the Civil War years.

Logan, Mary S., ed. Thirty Years in Washington. Hartford, 1901. Interesting series of anecdotes and reminiscences.

Lowry, Edward G. Washington Close-Ups: Intimate Views of Some Public Figures. Boston, 1921.

Lunberg, Emma O., and Milburn, Mary E. What Child Dependency Means in the District of Columbia And How It Can Be Prevented. Washington, 1924.

Mac Farland, Henry B.B. The Development of the District of Columbia. Washington, 1900. Old, but still useful study.

McCormick, Anne O'Hare. The World At Home. New York, 1956. Solid, interesting work on the workings of official Washington.

McMurray, Donald Le Crone. Coxey' Army, A Study of the Industiral Army Movement of 1894. Boston, 1929. Excellent work, containing much data about the march on Washington.

Mechlin, Leila. Works of Art in Washington. Washington, 1914. Detailed pictorial review of the great art works in the city up to 1914.

Miller, Charles A. Citizens Advisory Groups in the District of Columbia Government. Washington, 1961.

Moore, Joseph W. Picturesque Washington. Providence, 1884.

Murray, Robert K. Red Scare: A Study in National Hysteria, 1919-20.

Minneapolis, 1955. Very fine study containing much material on the effects of the Red Scare in the capital.

Nicolay, Helen. Our Capital on the Potomac. New York, 1924.

_____. Sixty Years of the Literary Society. Washington, 1934. Interesting history of the growth and accomplishments of one of Washington's most important cultural organizations.

O'Connor, Ellen M. Myrtilla Miner; A Memoir. New York, 1885. Quite old, but valuable in its treatment of one of the most important Washington female Negro leaders.

Odgers, M.M. Alexander Dallas Bache; Scientist and Educator, 1806-1867. Philadelphia, 1947. Solid, penetrating biography of an important Washington intellectual.

Oehser, Paul H. Sons of Science, The Story of the Smithsonian Institution and its Leaders. New York, 1949. The best work done on the great national hall of science and history.

Padover, Saul K. Thomas Jefferson and the National Capital. New York, 1946. The letters of Jefferson, describing the role he played in the development of Washington.

Porter, Sarah H. The Life and Times of Anne Royall. Cedar Rapids, Iowa, 1909. Amusing, interesting work on the famous social critic of the early nineteenth century.

Reps, John W. Monumental Washington: The Planning and Development of the Capitol Center. New York, 1967.

Sanderlin, Walter S. The Great National Project: A History of the Chesapeake and Ohio Canal, in The Johns Hopkins University Studies in Historical and Political Science. LXIV. no. 1 Baltimore, 1946.

Sands, Francis P.B, The Founders and Original Organizers of the Metropolitan Club, Washington, D.C. Washington, 1909.

Schmeckebier, Laurence. The District of Columbia, Its Government and Administration. Baltimore, 1928. An informative picture of the workings of all the District's complicated governmental machinery down through 1927.

Seaton, Josephine. William Winston Seaton of the National Intelligencer. Boston, 1871. Though somewhat biased, a good biography of the outstanding mayor of Washington. An up to date biography needs to be done.

Slauson, Allan B., ed. A History of the City of Washington, by the Washington Post. Washington, 1903.

Smith, Margaret Bayard. The First Forty Years of Washington Society, portrayed by the family letters of Mrs. Samuel Harrison Smith, ed., Galliard Hunt. New York, 1906. Perhaps the single richest source for the years prior to 1835.

Spaulding, Thomas M. The Literary Society in Peace and War. Washington, 1947.

Stern, Helen B., and Stein, Philip M. "O, Say Can You See?" A Bifocal Tour of Washington Washington, 1965. Very good study evaluating aspects of the racial question in the nation's capital.

Tucker, Glenn. Poltroons and Patriots: A Popular Account of the War of 1812. 2 vols. Indianapolis, 1954. Very readable study of this war, with much material concerning the burning and capture of Washington.

Tunnard, Christopher, and Reed, Henry. American Skyline: The Growth and Form of Our Cities and Towns. Boston, 1955. Contains valuable information on Washington's architectural development.

Washington Gas Light Company. Growing with Washington, the Story of Our First Hundred Years. Washington, 1948. Good history of the development of the city and the role of the Gas-Light Company in its growth.

Washington League of Women Voters. Washington D.C.; A Tale of Two Cities. Washington, 1962. Literate, provocative narrative of the city's historical development.

Washington Post. Ten Blocks From the White House: Anatomy of the Washington Riots of 1968. New York, 1968. Very good journalistic study of the riots after the assassination of Martin Luther King Jr.

Walsh, John J. Early Banks in the District of Columbia, 1792-1818. Washington, 1940.

Waters, Walter T., as told to William C. White. B.E.F.: The Whole Story of the Bonus Army. New York, 1933. First rate description of the "bonus army" march on Washington during the depression.

Weitzmann, Louis G. One Hundred Years of Catholic Charities in the District of Columbia. Washington, 1931.

Wharton, Anne H. Salons Colonial and Republican. Philadelphia, 1900.

_____. Social Life in the Early Republic. Philadelphia, 1902.

Whyte, James. The Uncivil War. New York, 1958.

Woodson, Carter G. The History of the Negro Church. Washington, 1945. Several good chapters on the development of the Negro churches in Washington.

Wright, Carroll D. The Economic Development of the District of Columbia. Washington, 1899.